How to Write Short Stories that Sell

How to write Short Stories that Sell

Writer's Digest Books
Cincinnati, Ohio 45242

Library of Congress Cataloging in Publication Data
Boggess, Louise.
  How to write short stories that sell.
  Includes index.
    1. Fiction—Authorship. 2. Short story.
I. Title.
PN3373.B58   808.3'1   79-26010
ISBN 0-89879-139-1

Design by Barron Krody

The two most engaging powers of an author are, to make new things familiar and familiar things new.

Samuel Johnson

Dedicated to my many students who helped me research and test these techniques.

Preface

A Memo to Short Story Writers

An impressive number of books have given aspiring writers instruction in fiction techniques. The majority of them approach the instruction by analyzing unrelated examples from published stories.

Instead, this book will give an over-the-shoulder look at the process successful writers use in developing a short story. You will begin with a salable idea and expand it step-by-step into a completed short story.

Anyone can easily learn this process by choosing an idea and working along with me. At each step I will analyze the essential techniques and suggest how to individualize them to your material.

If you carefully apply the information in this book, you will know the successful devices all professionals employ in writing short stories. Once you make this method your own, you can repeat the process in less time and with greater success.

I have thoroughly tested this method of writing short stories in my college classes, correspondence courses, educational television, short courses, workshops, and writer's conferences. Writers who used this method not only found it easy to follow, but it stimulated them to create new combinations from basic devices. They soon discovered that they wrote more emotionally, projected their plots and characters better, and consequently made repeated sales.

May you find in these pages the guidance and challenge you need to master the art of short story writing. When you make your first sale, I have accomplished the primary purpose of this book.

Louise Boggess

Contents

Creating Salable Ideas

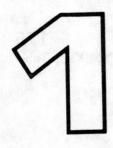

Almost everyone dreams of some day writing a short story that sells. In the short story you can create your own world and people it too. By remembering your own experiences and calling on your imagination, you can think of endless critical problems and believable solutions for your fictional characters. As you mentally write your short story, you picture the editor's enthusiasm and the reader's acclaim. You write another story and another—your success skyrockets!

But dreams like these pay off only if you make them a reality. Reality in the short story means learning how to write. A writer—exactly like a doctor or a lawyer—must learn the skills of his profession before he can apply his art or talent.

Anyone willing to invest the necessary time and effort can write a salable short story. This means you, even if you consistently put off writing until tomorrow or your filing cabinet already bulges with rejected manuscripts. Regardless of which category fits, you have already taken the first step in writing a short story: you have a desire to express yourself on paper.

Your next step consists of day-to-day discipline to

change your dream into reality. Push yourself beyond the satisfaction of merely putting words on paper or writing for your own pleasure, and accept the challenge of using professional techniques to communicate your emotional reactions to a larger audience.

Learning the craft of the short story demands concentration and work, but you have the ability. Good technique not only reduces the time lapse between your first attempt and your first sale, but it also earns dividends in personal satisfaction and in checks from the editor.

Successful writing, however, requires still another ingredient—self-confidence. Knock the gremlin of doubt from your shoulder and believe in yourself. Skillful writing not only gives you self-confidence, it also frees you to create and to better project your material.

Finally, you need a salable idea. Think of an idea as a sensation or emotional reaction to a person, place, or situation which suggests a story. Before we begin our study of ideas, file away for now in a safe place any old manuscripts—you may want to revise them later—and let's generate a new idea.

Incidents Generate Ideas

Occasionally you find a natural—an idea ready to plot into a short story. When this happens, the idea pushes you, dictating action almost faster than you can type it on paper.

A friend and collector made an appointment to see a person who advertised cut glass for sale. She visited with the woman for over an hour and eventually gave her a check for several pieces. The next day the police came to her with the check and explained the woman had been murdered. For days she could not recall a thing about the woman, so the detective asked her to go with him to the house. There she began to remember bits of conversation that helped catch the murderer. She wrote the story exactly as it happened—a natural.

Most of the time, however, you, the writer, must build the idea, so you start with a single incident that stimulates you. This stimulation can personally involve you, or it can come secondhand. Perhaps you react to something you heard on the radio, saw on television, or read. If you find you keep recalling this incident, you should go to work on it.

When a professional writer wants to expand an incident into an idea, he applies the essentials of a short story: plot, setting, characters, time, theme, or gimmick-symbol. To create an idea, write each of these fundamentals at the top of separate sheets of paper. Place your incident on the appropriate sheet. You'll see what I mean if you work right along with me while I develop an idea from an incident that happened to me.

Recently a promoter of antiques shows invited me to set up an American cut glass exhibit at the fairgrounds in San Francisco. On the day before the show opened, I checked in at the desk and received my space assignment. I noticed that the space number differed from the one previously sent me.

"Yesterday morning," the woman explained, "they shifted us from our regular building to this annex. We had to change all the space numbers." She directed me to drive to the first large door at the back of the building. "You can take your car inside to unload. The men in blue overalls will get the display tables for you."

When I reached my assigned area, someone else

occupied the space—a simple error we quickly corrected as I took the unoccupied adjacent space. While I set up the exhibit, this mix-up kept coming to my mind. It suggested a possible problem for a plot—as well as a setting for a short story.

1. Plot

On the plot sheet write this sentence: "Two people get assigned the same space at an antiques show."

Most stories open on the day of the problem—the day when a situation occurs that forces the major character to find an immediate solution. A problem may result from the pressure of time, the effects of environment, conflict with other characters, or the indecisiveness of the major character. The major character makes one attempt after another to solve the problem. This series of events produces the plot of the story.

To expand the problem, apply the magic words *suppose*, *perhaps*, and *what if*. *Suppose* that a single man and a single girl in their twenties receive the same assignment for a large space at an antiques show. *Perhaps* the shift to a smaller building left no other space available. *What if* neither brought enough antiques to fill the larger space? So they agree to share it. Now think of the setting.

2. Setting

Jot down on the setting page: "antiques show."

A short story takes place in a basic setting, such as a town, a school campus, a public park, a state fair, or an office. Since a central location gives unity to the story, try to contain the entire action in as small an area as possible. The setting may dominate the action of the story, help the reader to identify with the major character, or merely form the background. If possible, choose a setting that will provide or intensify the character conflict described in the story.

Setting up for an antiques show can be as exciting as the bustle backstage at a Broadway show on opening night. Vans and pickups drive inside the building, unloading cartons of antiques at assigned spaces. Laughter and shouts of greeting mingle with the banging of display tables and honking cars. Little by little the various exhibits take shape for the opening next day.

I wrote down numerous sensory impressions on the setting sheet: "the rough cement floor, the echo of voices in a large building, the chilling fog, the smell of exhaust fumes from cars, and the aroma of perking coffee." I will work all of these in later to project the background of the story, but don't expect to put down all your sensory reactions at one sitting.

3. Characters

The basic short story uses at least three characters: a *major* and two *supporting*. One supporting character helps the major character solve the problem, while the other supporting character hinders the solution. You must know the solution to the problem in order to assign the proper functions to the supporting characters. The character who helps reach the solution functions as the *positive supporting* character. The other functions as the *negative supporting* character. Naturally, you'll also create some minor characters later as you expand the plot.

At this point we need to know the age, sex, background, and problem typical of characters that appear in magazine stories. If you analyze a cross section of current magazine short stories, you will find that many of them focus on the problem of a single person involved in a love triangle. Very few contain no love interest.

Applying this analysis, I chose a single woman as the major character. Few women can write convincingly as a man, and relatively few men can write with conviction as a woman. Name the characters early so that you begin to think of them as real people. Natalee seems to project the old-fashioned yet young feminine image I want for the major character's name. Baxter adds stability to the given name.

Recently a dealer told me her partner died of cancer. At that particular show she decided to see if she could continue the business alone. She had been tied up in probate court getting possession of the merchandise.

Suppose that Natalee and her Aunt Harriet owned antiques and operated from an old Victorian home in San Francisco. They sold from the house only by appointment but did most of the business exhibiting at one show after another. I see them specializing in glass and old china—mostly small items—at shows and probably displaying furniture at the house. I know several dealers who operate this way. After her aunt's sudden death and probation of the will, Natalee plans to decide at this show whether or not to sell the antiques business or to continue running it alone.

At a dinner party a very aggressive and successful young man told me that he found many of his real-estate prospects by reading the obituary columns. As soon as he could sell the antiques and Victorian house his wife inherited, he would use the money to open his own real estate firm.

Suppose that a young and aggressive real estate

salesman calls to see if Natalee might sell the house after her aunt's death. Let's name him Kenneth Preston. He begins to date her regularly and suggests that they get married as soon as he can buy into a real estate partnership. He offers to find buyers and help her liquidate her antiques. She can do better, he urges, investing her money in real estate.

At another show I met a man in his mid twenties who put himself through college and law school buying and selling in flea markets. Let's make Steve Atkins a struggling new lawyer who partially supports his own law office by selling paper goods, toys, and other small items at antiques shows.

I see Steve as an extremely reliable person not likely to take advantage of others. By contrast, Kenneth, a manipulator, plans his own future at the expense of others.

The aunt reared Natalee and sent her to college. Very likely she majored in interior decorating. Through study and working with the aunt, Natalee has learned a great deal about antiques. So Natalee and these two men form the love triangle.

On the character sheet write: "Natalee Baxter, major character, antiques dealer; Steve Atkins, positive supporting character, a new lawyer who deals in antiques; Kenneth Preston, negative supporting character, a successful real estate salesman."

4. Time

Try to keep the short story within a brief span of time—hours, days, a week. *Immediacy* refers to the time limit of the story. The shorter the immediacy, the stronger the suspense.

The action of the story begins on a Friday afternoon when Natalee goes to set up, and ends on Sunday afternoon near the closing of the show. A *flashback*— discussed in detail in Chapter 5—refers to the events that took place before the story opened. Flashbacks will cover events before that fateful Friday afternoon in Natalee's life.

On the time sheet put "three days," the average duration of an antiques show.

5. Theme

Every short story has a message for the reader called a *theme*. Many writers find that a pithy saying, an old adage, or a slogan starts the imagination working. But make sure to personalize the theme to the major character and the problem.

By knowing the theme, you can move your major character forward and backward toward the solution of the problem, and can keep her shifting between the negative and positive trait.

Steve offers Natalee love with the opportunity to work together for financial security. Kenneth promises an implied financial security, with love secondary to career. Since Natalee will choose Steve, we write this theme on the sheet: "Sometimes you must listen to your heart instead of your head."

6. Gimmick-symbol

Not all stories contain a gimmick or symbol. A *gimmick* refers to a physical object that assists in causing the trouble and later in solving it. When the major character endows this object with a spiritual power, you have a *symbol*. Since our story deals with selling antiques, certainly some piece of old glass or china should serve as the gimmick.

Dealers worry constantly about buying a fake or reproduction for the genuine article. Many modern craftsmen have reproduced vases that closely resemble those made by Tiffany at the turn of the century. Everyone knows the name of Tiffany. On the gimmick-symbol sheet write: "small genuine Tiffany vase."

See how easily you can generate an idea from a stimulating incident and from knowing the essentials of the short story? Don't expect to build an idea in a matter of minutes. Frankly, I spent a number of days working on the Natalee idea. But I can assure you that the more ideas you have generated with this method, the less time the next idea will take.

The time has come for you to go to work. Choose an incident, place it on the correct sheet, and develop it into an idea. When you have an idea, you take the next forward step in writing your short story.

Can You Sum it Up in Three Lines?

Writers have learned to compact an idea into a three-sentence formula that helps to organize thoughts. Let's apply this formula to our idea:

1. *Name the major character, problem, setting, and immediacy:*

Natalee Baxter must decide by the end of an antiques show whether or not she will sell her antiques business.

2. *Tell which character will help and which will hinder solving the problem:*

Steve Atkins wants her as his girl friend and partner in antiques—later marriage. Kenneth Preston wants her to sell the antiques and invest in a real estate partnership for him so they will have financial security when they marry.

3. Give the outcome of the story and the theme:

Natalee falls in love with Steve and decides not to sell She learns that sometimes you must listen to your heart instead of your head.

Apply the formula to your idea. If you have written a page or two on each step, you have not really firmed up the idea. Continue to work on the summary until you can fit it into this brief formula. Whether you discover a natural or develop your idea with the essentials of the short story, either way you still must test it for sales potential.

Testing Story Ideas

Some writers have developed unique screening systems. One suspense writer I know insists that the hair stands up on the back of her neck whenever she gets a salable idea. An author of love stories confides she gets a lump in her throat when she finds an unusually good idea. A prolific mystery writer swears he gets an electric shock with a surefire idea.

Unfortunately, few of us have these extrasensory perceptions. We must rely on more orthodox methods and test our ideas by the critical standards of an editor.

1. Enthusiasm

Only you know if you feel enthusiastic about an idea. Do you rush to the typewriter and not want to leave it? Do you feel excited about your characters, look forward to meeting them in action, and think of numerous complications that demand decisions? A "yes" to these questions guarantees your enthusiasm for an idea.

Unless an idea inspires and challenges you to give it your creative best, discard it. You might as well write between each line of your story, "I have no enthusiasm for this idea."

Do not mistake sentimentality for enthusiasm. Sometimes a writer becomes so attached to an idea through long hours of trying to develop it into a story that he not only refuses to discard it, but will balk at parting with a single precious word. To sell, you must put aside all sentimentality for tired or threadbare ideas. Either give them a shot of life with a fresh approach or get rid of them.

Anytime you lose your enthusiasm for a challenging idea, put it aside, do more research, try a new approach, or invest more creative thinking time. A woman who worked on a short story for several months admitted she lost her enthusiasm at intervals. But each time she recalled the incident which stimulated the idea, she became so excited she worked twice as hard. So possibly this method will help you regenerate enthusiasm for an idea.

Do I feel enthusiastic about the Natalee idea? I know how forlorn and alone Natalee can feel, exhibiting at the first show after her aunt's death. Suave Kenneth will think of so many ways to get her to sell the antiques, how can Steve possibly make her see the truth in such a short time? I must find the answer in the show itself. I jog my memory for other incidents that happened at various shows. I feel so enthusiastic I want to stop writing this book and go to work on the story.

2. Theme

When I first decided to write fiction, a selling author offered to help me develop an idea into a story. "Now tell me what you want to say in one short sentence," he directed.

I thought he had lost his mind. I handed him three typewritten pages.

"If you need this many words, you don't know what you want to say," he summed up and ended the interview.

A *theme* summarizes in one brief sentence what the major character learned from the events of the story. This sentence usually comes near the end. Often a strong theme will linger indefinitely in the reader's memory long after he has forgotten the events. Strive to give your theme this kind of power.

Juvenile and women's magazines stress the theme so strongly that they want you to spell it out. In some magazines the story carries the theme in italics to emphasize its importance. Stories for science fiction, men's magazines, and the quality market imply the theme, letting the reader word his own. Even the most enigmatic literary story has some kind of implied theme.

We want to state the theme strongly in our example story. Natalee's lack of confidence in operating the antiques business alone, combined with Kenneth's helpfulness since her aunt's death, stacks things in his favor. But Steve, by forcing her to face the fact that she knows nothing but antiques as a way of life, shows he really cares about her. Although she admires Kenneth's confidence and success, she eventually realizes that love comes from the heart. So we easily summarize what she learns from the events of the story in this sentence: "Sometimes you must listen to your heart instead of your head."

3. Emotional conflict

A good idea suggests conflict—the heartbeat of a

story. All stories contain two types of conflict: *inner* and *outer*.

Since the major character has a *trait* with a negative and positive facet, the struggle between the two for dominance provides the inner conflict. The outer conflict—also called *character conflict*—results when the major character expresses this inner turmoil by agreeing or disagreeing with the other characters. In most stories the major character's problem and resulting decisions develop the inner and outer conflict of the story.

Some stories use a third type of conflict that develops from an unusual setting. In one type of setting conflict, a character struggles against the forces of nature. A man, for example, may get lost in the desert and struggle to find his way back to civilization. In a suspense story, an old Victorian house that holds the key to a mystery may create another type of conflict from a setting.

Believable conflict, regardless of the type, holds the reader's attention.

Let's look at our idea for conflict. Two men want the same girl, so we have character conflict. The girl feels torn between selling and keeping the antiques business—the inner conflict. The mix-up in space assignments starts conflict from the setting—a conflict that will affect the minor characters. So the Natalee idea suggests conflict in love, career, and setting.

4. Reader appeal

Some readers prefer stories dealing with situations similar to their own. The young mother finds comfort in the fact that others have dirty dishes stacked in the sink, piles of soiled clothes on the laundry-room floor, unexpected guests for dinner, or a forgotten appointment. Many readers enjoy *self-identification*.

Other readers seek to escape from their humdrum life. The quiet little file clerk reads of big-game hunting or diving for lost treasure. The exhausted mother escapes into the glamorous world of the fashion model or the movie starlet. All these people seek *escape* from their true identity.

The more readers you reach, the better your market possibilities. Discard any idea so specialized in scope that it will interest only a few readers; concentrate on those ideas which attract a large number in self-identification and escape. Our story provides self-identification through romance and escape through the antiques setting. The story takes the reader behind the scenes to see the preparations and inner action at an antiques show.

5. *Plus Value*

A *plus value* means any special quality that removes the story from the commonplace or routine and increases the marketing possibilities. Writers achieve a plus value with a unique problem, clever dialogue, strong plot, a sentimental gimmick, or a symbol readers can identify with. A reversal of the accepted adds a surprise quality. Dynamic characterization excites the reader. Firsthand knowledge of a special background or detailed research assure authenticity. Writers constantly rejuvenate banal ideas by injecting a plus value.

Constantly analyze your writing for a plus value. You may find that you give every story the same plus value. On the other hand, you may change the plus value with each new effort. One story may reveal knowledge of strange cults, while another may feature a penetrating mood. The plus value must always expand—never limit—the market.

Our idea focuses on the love triangle and the background of the antiques show. My personal knowledge of antiques, shows, and the professional lingo adds a plus value of authenticity.

6. Market

A good idea will sell to a number of markets. As in nonfiction magazine articles, the market for the short story has become highly specialized. No longer do you find general magazines that take all types of stories; rather, you must look for the specialty market and tailor your idea to it. These magazines, like the tide, wax and wane—dominate the market for a while, then fade in popularity. So to stay on top of the changing market, you must constantly check with Writer's Market and the two professional monthlies, Writer's Digest and The Writer.

The past few years have seen an expanding market in science fiction. The murder mystery has diversified from the old "who dunit" into the locked-room puzzle of the "how dunit" and the psychological story of the "why dunit." The suspense story has risen to great popularity, appearing in the dress of the gothic, the spy, the horror, occult, or adventure. The confession magazines offer beginners a special opportunity to earn while they learn.

The quality or literary magazines continue to buy stories that present a segment of real life. The religious market likes stories that involve decisive moments, powerful themes, or making the right choices in life. Editors for women's magazines buy stories of romance, family conflicts, or marital difficulties.

Chapter 11 discusses the specifics of marketing, but we can mention here that love creeps into almost any type of story. The detective may want to prove the lovely heroine did not kill her husband, or the man in outer space must choose between love and returning to his home planet. A lost love often dominates the quality market. No one can truly eliminate love from the suspense categories.

The Natalee story will go to one of the women's magazines.

You will want to test your ideas step by step, exactly as I did the one about Natalee. Testing ideas eliminates tired thinking and alerts you to new and exciting events. If your idea seems weak in any of the above six tests, work on that part now. You can always think of a stronger theme, build up the emotional conflict, broaden the reader appeal, or add another plus value.

From here on we will develop the Natalee idea through a step-by-step process to a completed short story. I chose a love story because it involves the basic techniques that all categories use. You'll find the love story the easiest to write and the quickest to sell. Once you know how to write a love story, you can easily adapt the method to any specialty market. Finally, you will learn how familiarity with an interesting setting can add freshness to the old love triangle and make the story sell.

At this point you should have your idea ready to work along with me. Do not jump ahead in the book until you have satisfactorily applied each illustrated technique to your own idea. To check your progress from chapter to chapter, compare what you learned today with what you knew yesterday. If some of the terms seem unfamiliar or confusing, don't worry. Soon they will become old friends, and useful aids. Ideas begin their journey to salability when you work them into a good *plot summary.*

Plot—Choices and Consequences

A salable short story must have a believable plot. Since plotting means linking one event to the next, most successful writers follow a basic formula or plot skeleton. To create drama in the sequence of events and conflict between characters, the formula starts with a problem the reader can identify with; then the major character must eventually provide a plausible solution.

A Sure-fire Formula

The fiction formula, developed and tested through the years by writers and editors, divides the story action into four parts: (1) the *problem situation*, which ends with a *decision*; (2) the *complications*, which end on a *decision*; (3) the *crisis*, followed by the moment of *revelation*; and (4) the *climax* with a statement of the *theme*.

The salable short story carefully balances these various sections. Think of the average short story covering twenty double-spaced typewritten pages, or approximately 5,000 words. The best balance for the formula allots five pages to the problem situation, eight to the complications, five to the crisis, and two to the climax. These page proportions serve also as a basis for approximating other lengths. A 3,000-word story—about twelve or thirteen pages—would run 3-6-3-l.

Remember, these figures only approximate the lengths. Lengths go in cycles. The market that buys the 5,000-word story also features a short-short. Magazines that do not buy short-shorts vary the story length from 2,000 to 4,000 words. In the final analysis let your material and the market suggest the proportions. Even though you vary the distribution slightly, you must still maintain the delicate balance of the divisions, so that the drama builds gradually to a crisis point.

The pages of your short story unfold the action for the reader exactly as in a movie, stage play, or television drama. In your story, however, your words must create the pictures and suggest the sound effects that feed the reader's imagination.

1. Problem situation

In the first five pages, the problem situation introduces the characters, describes the setting, and establishes a problem. A major character must solve the problem within a short time span called an *immediacy*. The story action must revolve around this major character and his efforts to find the right or best solution to the problem.

What causes the problem depends on whether you emphasize the major character's trait, the situation, or both. A *trait* refers to a distinguishing quality or characteristic. If, for example, your major character acts impulsively, too generously, or indecisively, any of these traits can create a problem.

When the trait causes the problem, shape the plot action to the character. A woman, for instance, blames another child for the accident that injured her son's eye and seeks revenge. Her trait of revenge creates the action.

Sometimes a set of circumstances creates a problem for the character. A man comes home to find his wife and son murdered. He determines to help the police find the killer. If the situation causes the problem, develop the characters to fit the action.

Any story that combines a good reader-identification situation with strong characterization sells quickly.

Introduce one character at a time in relation to the problem of the major one. If at all possible, bring in the positive supporting character first and then the negative one.

You may need minor characters to increase the conflict. If you can't get them on scene in person during the problem situation, at least let another character mention them by name or profession. The minor characters should develop naturally from the setting and the action of the story. We can't get the Larkins in the opening scene, but we let Kenneth tell Natalee about them.

To further intensify the character conflict, bring in a gimmick or symbol if one fits naturally into the plot. Remember that the gimmick or symbol must assist in creating conflict and in solving it. Finally, make the setting contribute to the character conflict.

The problem situation ends by confronting the major character with a choice of action, and he makes a negative decision in that it moves him away from the real solution to the problem. The major character believes this choice will solve the problem, but you, the author, know it will lead him astray and create a complication. If the decision solves the problem, you have no story.

We learn best by doing. Let's apply these techniques

to the problem situation for the Natalee story. To write the plot summary, we must adapt our idea to the formula. Here and there we'll add information and characters. This adaptation to the formula will give only the skeleton plot or the bare bones. The elaboration covering the bones with flesh will come in later chapters when we block out the scenes.

We must put pressure on Natalee to sell. Suppose Kenneth learns he can buy into a real estate firm if he can secure the necessary funds. He puts pressure on Natalee to sell the antiques and finds a minor character who might buy them.

Many decorators sell antiques, and some have set up small shops in conjunction with their business. Perhaps Kenneth met the Larkins when they decorated a model home for a new area where he sold houses. Without consulting her, he makes a date with them to see Natalee's antiques. Naturally, he chose the evening Natalee must set up for the show. Summarize the **problem situation** this way:

> In preparing to set up for an antiques show Natalee Baxter discovers she has the same space number as Steve Atkins. The two finally agree to share the area as neither brought enough stock to fill a large space. While she unpacks the Tiffany vase, Kenneth Preston comes by to tell her he has an opportunity to buy into a real estate firm but needs to raise more money. He has arranged for her to meet the Larkins, possible buyers, at her house that night and warns her to arrive on time. Natalee barely gets unpacked and partially set up when she must leave. Steve offers to finish the job.
>
> **Decision**: Natalee agrees after giving Steve some directions and hurries to meet Kenneth.

This decision favors selling the business and moves her away from the solution, which is to continue to sell antiques with Steve.

2. Complications

Each new problem develops from the previous decision. The number of complications depends on the strength of the problem and on the major character's trait. A twenty-page story normally requires three complications, developed over a space of eight pages. The complications vary in emotional intensity as well as in word length, so distribute them as your material indicates.

To create complications, take a pad and pencil and list the possibilities. Go back to the essentials of the short story for help. You may discover a complication in the setting, the gimmick, or the traits of the characters.

Sometimes research on a part of the story supplies a good complication. A show promoter mentioned that he forced all dealers to label any reproductions of antiques. This suggested turning the story on the identification of a reproduction.

When you have listed a number of complications, choose the best three. The decisions at the end of these complications must change the character from the way you introduced him in the problem situation.

Do not make all the decisions negative and have the character change miraculously at the conclusion. The complication decisions must move the major character gradually toward the chosen solution. In other words, let the character take a long step toward the solution with a right decision and then go backward with a negative decision. Make the negative step back shorter than the positive step so that the major character gradually moves closer to the solution.

Since the initial decision of the problem situation sets the character on the wrong course, the complication choices must create a balance. You may follow any sequence as long as you end up with one more right than wrong decision.

To reenforce a negative/positive balance, give both supporting characters the same amount of time with the major character. In each complication scene show equally the negative and positive side of the major character's trait. The crisis then upsets this balance for a final outcome.

Let's develop the complications for the Natalee story. To make Natalee's problem worse, she has trouble starting her old station wagon. She operates on a very tight budget since she can't sell anything until after probation of the will. We need another minor character or two to balance the negative function of the Larkins. Kenneth has sold an old Victorian home to the Crandalls, a young couple who inherited a large sum of money. He hopes to earn a commission by getting the Larkins to decorate it:

Complication 1: Natalee has trouble starting her old station wagon and arrives minutes before the Larkins. Kenneth reminds her of his opportunity to buy into a real estate firm. As soon as he can buy in, they can get married. But the Larkins admit they do not have the money to buy at present. If they could bring the Crandalls and let them select items they want, the Larkins might get the decorating job and could buy all the chosen items.

Decision: Kenneth persuades Natalee to go along with his plan.

This negative decision moves Natalee away from the selected solution. But then comes another development:

Complication 2: The next day Natalee gets upset with Steve when she finds he has mixed the antiques but kept her shop sign, Heritage House Antiques. During the day she gets to know him and feels a strange attraction she can't explain to herself. When she leaves, she can't start the car. Steve suggests that he drive her home and get a friend of his to take care of the car.

Decision: Natalee accepts his offer.

This positive decision moves Natalee a long way toward the solution.

Complication 3: Natalee and Steve arrive late for the appointment. Steve insists on coming inside to help. Kenneth tries to get rid of Steve. The Crandalls listen to Steve identify the various antiques as to their relative value, and the Larkins grow visibly upset. Kenneth tells Natalee to get rid of Steve before he blows the deal. Natalee suggests Steve call his friend about the car. Alone with Natalee, he warns that the Larkins and Kenneth plan to take advantage of her and the Crandalls. He asks if Kenneth intends to collect a finder's fee. Natalee doesn't know who or what to believe.

Decision: Natalee promises Steve she will delay selling anything to the Larkins.

While this decision makes her more positive, it only creates the necessary balance between Natalee's positive and negative facet for the crisis to upset.

3. Crisis

The crisis, the worst complication, that happens to the major character, opens with a dark or black moment when the major character can see no possible way to solve the problem. The character stands to lose everything. The crisis action moves quickly to the end of the immediacy, forcing the character to choose the positive solution.

The interaction of the two supporting characters finally results in the positive answer, when the major character experiences a **moment of revelation**. At this point the character sees the right solution and undergoes a change. The *trait* or the *seriousness* of the problem situation determines the amount of change, varying from recognition of a human frailty to the promise of great reform.

The major character must always solve the problem for the upbeat ending or fail to find the answer for the downbeat one. Never let a supporting character solve the problem for the major character. By all means avoid the amateur trick of bringing in a new character in the crisis to solve the problem.

Any time you let your major character sit and only think through the change, you write a come-to-realize story that won't sell. Neither may you solve the problem with an act of God—a storm, death, or an accident—unless you previously point to such a happening. Do not let a minor character's experience which parallels that of the major character provide the solution.

Once the major character experiences a moment of revelation and changes from the person you first introduced in the story, the crisis ends.

In the crisis for the Natalee story the gimmick must help her choose the right solution. The action of the two men forces the moment of revelation and her character change. We return to the setting of the problem situation. The crisis develops in this way:

Natalee feels a very low dark moment. She has angered Kenneth, probably lost the sale to the Larkins—all because of Steve; and she has not sold as much at the show as she expected. To make matters worse, the car needs such expensive repairs that the mechanic recommended she buy a van he has at a bargain price. She even begins to doubt Kenneth's love. Steve tries to talk her into a partnership.

Kenneth arrives before closing time and explains that

the Crandalls called him and will arrive soon. They want her to authenticate some of the items the Larkins left for the Crandalls to consider. The sale depends on Natalee's authentication.

The Crandalls arrive and show a fake Tiffany vase the Larkins represented as genuine. She knows that she cannot identify a fake as the genuine article [moment of revelation].

Natalee has now reached the point of making the decision that leads her to the solution you planned.

4. Climax

The **climax** usually continues the crisis. Anticlimax results when you let the climax occur a day or two after the crisis. Bring the major character and the positive supporting one together for the upbeat ending. The major character has found the right solution and summarizes what he or she has learned from the events of the story. Give the major character the reward he thought he had lost and wind up the story quickly.

While an upbeat ending offers a better opportunity to sell, you do have some choices. With the happy ending the major character solves the problem and attains the goal. To prevent a predictable ending, add a surprise twist—but only one which you have already pointed out as a possibility in a previous scene. Never startle or shock your reader by withholding facts the major character knows or by bringing in new information. Certainly do not introduce a new character at the last minute to give the final outcome.

In some stories the major character works toward achieving a certain goal but exchanges it for a more unselfish one. We call this the *altered-goal* ending. For the *meaningful* or *satisfying* ending, the major character fails to attain the goal but learns a fact that will help him live a better life. The reader realizes the story could not have ended any other way. With a true *circle* ending, the character does not change his trait or solve the problem.

In the women's magazines, the character usually has a better understanding of how to handle the problem in the future. But you can end on implication. State early in the story that a certain event will happen with specific results. The event occurs, and the reader supplies the ending. A wife knows that if her husband remembers their anniversary, their marriage will survive. Long-stem red roses arrive.

Sometimes the way the characters act in the climax leads the reader to improvise the happy ending. Television with its time restrictions has popularized the implication ending.

So far we have discussed only upbeat endings. The literary or quality story may let the character go from bad to worse with no actual solution. But overall, stories with downbeat endings sell poorly and at times for less money.

The Natalee story will end on the implication that she will eventually marry Steve:

Climax: Kenneth leaves in a huff. The Crandalls thank her and ask her to help them do their decorating. Steve slips an arm around Natalee, and she knows that sometimes you must listen to your heart instead of your head.

Once you have developed your idea through the plot formula, you may see places that need research. Almost every short story needs some research, even though you do no more than talk with friends who handle work similar to that which you have designated for a character. Perhaps you want to check on a setting or some legal procedure which adds authenticity to the story. When you write about what you know, you eliminate much research. Yet good research does much to sell a story. If you need do any research, do it before you write the plot summary, as you might find some interesting complications.

Choose a Salable Pattern

A *pattern* indicates an adaptation of the general formula to your specific material and the market. Through the years writers and editors have created certain basic patterns that vary the story emphasis.

Eventually you will favor one particular pattern and improvise some variations for your material. You may want to combine parts of two patterns and create a different one, as other writers have done. Even in this creative venture, you work from the basic formula. To choose the best pattern for your idea, acquire a working knowledge of the basic ones:

1. *Situation pattern*

This pattern follows the formula exactly but builds the story action around the problem situation. You then create the characters to fit the situation.

Let's go back to the idea of the man who found his wife and son murdered. At the end of the problem situation he calls the police. In the complications he tries various means of flushing out the killer. At the beginning of the crisis he almost admits failure but decides to bait a trap with his own life. The trap catches the murderer. The climax shows his satisfaction in stopping the person from killing others and in bringing him to justice.

Almost all categories of short stories continually plot fiction with the situation pattern. Examine your idea and see if it emphasizes situation. If it does not, then look for another pattern, emphasizing character.

2. Character pattern

The character pattern follows the formula, but the trait of the major character provokes the problem and shapes the story action. Open the story with the major character acting strongly in the negative, but not so strongly as to prevent a believable change.

Several different devices will assist you in spotlighting the major character's trait: open with three incidents that focus on it; let the character explain his actions to the reader; or involve the major character in conflict with the other characters.

Go back to the idea of the mother who wants to avenge her son's loss of sight. In the problem situation, her husband urges her to forget the accident, but she decides to make the boy suffer. In various complications she tries to exclude him from association with his peers. At the crisis the boy tries to kill himself, and she must talk him out of jumping to his death. In the climax she learns that revenge only brings more tragedy.

Any confession story, like the one outlined above, always builds from the *character trait*. When the same spy or detective appears in a series of stories, the plot often stresses the character trait. Many writers for science fiction, religious, and women's magazines plot from character trait.

3. Biter-bit pattern

While this pattern emphasizes character trait, it develops a very unsympathetic character with a weakness which will trap him in the climax. In short, the biter gets bit. By all means work out the trap ending before you plot the rest of the story. Once you know the trap, build a strong problem situation to show the negative trait. The length of time for the action may vary from hours to months. Keep the complications short so you can move rapidly to the crisis and spring the trap in the climax. Exit quickly, using implication.

What if an illegal alien prides himself on always finding the cheaper way? He lives with an American citizen in her apartment. To stop deportation, he marries her, but only in the cheaper civil ceremony. He has the reception at her apartment and talks her out of a honeymoon. When he meets a girl with a larger apartment, a better job, and a car, he decides to divorce his wife. In the crisis he gets the cheaper and faster annulment and moves in with the new girl. The climax reveals that the annulment returned him to his illegal status.

You'll find a biter-bit fun to write, but only the clever ones sell, mainly to the men's market. Occasionally you see one in the literary or detective magazine. Beginners would do better to think in terms of the situation or character pattern.

4. Slice-of-life pattern

While this pattern follows the formula exactly, it combines a weak character trait with trivial incidents from life. The literary or quality story holds a mirror up to life and reports the results. Weak decisions lead to a very slight character change. This pattern has recently infiltrated some of the women's magazines. For this particular market the story requires a stronger than usual plot plus a believable character change. The story may or may not state the theme.

A story for the women's market would open with a newly-divorced father picking up his son for a first visiting day. He has made elaborate plans that begin with new clothes, a trip to the beach, and dinner at a special cafe for children. The complications reverse his plans: the clothes don't fit, the rain ruins the beach trip, and the son gets sick. In the crisis the boy cries and wants assurance the father will continue the visiting day. For the climax, the father assures the boy that spending the day together means more to him than anything else in life.

This type of story takes a mastery of technique to build strong emotion from trivial events and maintain a forward movement to an important outcome. Save this pattern for the future when you have sold several stories.

5. Circle pattern

In this pattern the climax overlaps the problem situation, implying that events will repeat themselves. Your material helps you decide on the overlap: the character trait, the situation, or a combination of both.

The circle deviates from the basic situation or character pattern in the middle of the climax so as to return to the problem situation. Instead of making the major character establish the change, you confront him with a situation similar to that found at the opening. The character nullifies the change to unite the circle.

Commercial writers have tried to expand the market for this quality pattern by giving the major character a slight change. While the character does not actually change the trait or situation, he does see the problem more clearly. Another adaptation transfers the trait or situation to another character. When a similar event occurs, another character comes forward and assumes the role originally held by the major character. The major character changes and realizes that the cycle of events will repeat itself.

Suppose a man wins a large sum of money in a sweepstake. When asked what he plans to do with the money, he says first he will quit his job. In the complications he buys a big car, a large home, custom-made clothes, and so on. At the crisis he has not only spent all the money but owes almost as much. In the climax he goes to the sweepstake office to spend his last dollar on a ticket only to witness a new winner receiving a big check. The new winner says to a reporter, "First, I'll quit my job." The latest winner will probably repeat the chain of events—the implication ending.

The literary or quality market favors this pattern. Occasionally in the women's magazines you find a light humorous story dealing with a family situation. The character fails to change the trait but does recognize that most people do not see their own weakness.

The biter-bit, the slice-of-life, and the circle pattern require not only experience in writing, but also a specialized idea. Stay in the mainstream with the situation, character trait, or a combination of the two until you know your craft of writing. All story patterns must promise the reader conflict to hold his interest, immediacy to excite him, suspense to keep him guessing, plausibility to make him believe, and continuity to keep him reading to the very end.

At this point you should have mentally tested your idea with all the patterns and should tentatively have chosen one. Before you make a final decision, however, note that the plot summary of the Natalee story used to illustrate the formula combines character trait and situation—this combination sells best today. As soon as you complete the plot summary for your idea, you will develop the *viewpoint character*.

Viewpoint—The Emotional Focus

Imagine yourself an editor who picks up this unsolicited short story to read:

> The little group cluttered one corner of the airport lounge. Janice wondered why she had been so stupid to come and to so completely reveal her true feelings. Paul rubbed at a speck of dust on the camera lens and wished he could get rid of the man who had wrecked his marriage. Lee mentally worded his resignation as a press agent, for he was finished if that has-been actress didn't show up for this publicity stunt.

A story belongs to the character who dominates the action. In this opening paragraph the author wanders in and out of the minds of three different characters, creating total confusion. This story belongs to no one in particular. You, like the editor, would stop reading right there and quickly clip a standard rejection slip to the manuscript. Yes, editors daily receive short stories where the author has not learned the simple but effective techniques of viewpoint.

Viewpoint means the emotional focus from which you project the action of the story. *Objective* viewpoint merely reports the facts unemotionally without going into the mind of any character. Since the short story requires strong emotion, you write in *subjective* viewpoint.

A Choice of Viewpoints

In subjective viewpoint, you share the thoughts of one or more characters with the reader. By knowing what a character thinks and feels, the reader identifies emotionally with him and becomes involved in the action. The action develops around a major character called the *Viewpoint*. The type of subjective viewpoint you select determines the amount of emotion and the degree of dramatic continuity. Most short stories project the action through *single major character* viewpoint.

1. Single major character

In this type of subjective viewpoint, only the major character shares his thoughts and reactions with the reader. Try to introduce the major viewpoint character in the first sentence of the story:

> I parked the old station wagon near the entrance of the exhibition building and sat quietly for a moment to compose myself. If I could get through this antiques show, I might find the right answer to selling the business. I climbed out of the car and walked resolutely to the check-in desk to get my space number.

If you write the story from Steve Atkins' viewpoint, you make Natalee a positive supporting character. Both have the same general problem—someone to love:

> Steve Atkins parked the new van in the building near his assigned space, a little surprised at the large space. As he unloaded cartons of antiques, he didn't feel the old excitement of setting up. Lately, his life seemed at a standstill. He wanted to reach out for something but didn't know what.

Once you step inside the viewpoint character, all reactions and thoughts belong to him. You need not clutter the story by constantly reestablishing the viewpoint with "he said," "he heard," or "he felt." The reader does not need these constant reminders, for he has merged with the viewpoint character.

An exception does exist. When you write several long paragraphs of thoughts or inner conflict with little or no action—as when the viewpoint character argues with himself—reestablish the viewpoint periodically with an occasional "he reasoned," "he thought," or "he wished."

Single major character viewpoint adapts easily to either first or third person. If you choose third person, put the thoughts also in third person, not first. The exception, however, provides that if you wish the third-person viewpoint character to think of an important fact which points to later action, put the thoughts in first person and, if necessary, add quotation marks. Do insert a "he thought." Use this device sparingly, however, or you spoil the effectiveness. Otherwise, never put quotation marks on thoughts to give the appearance of dialogue.

Whether you write in first or third person depends on several factors. The first person offers easy characterization, strong emotion, and fast reader identification. Some writers find third person more difficult to write, as they cannot step easily into the character. So these professionals find they create better emotion by writing in first person and then changing it later to third. If you have established viewpoint correctly, then change only the pronoun from first to third person, as in this illustration:

Natalee Baxter parked the old station wagon near the entrance of the exhibition building and sat quietly for a moment to compose herself. If she could get through this antiques show, she might find the right answer to selling the business. She climbed out of the car and walked resolutely to the check-in desk to get her space number.

In the final analysis consider your character, the plot, and the market before you choose the personal pronoun.

A majority of the magazine short stories favor single major character viewpoint, either first or third person. This type of viewpoint provides strong continuity, instant reader identification, and dramatic suspense. It adapts easily to any word length, setting, gimmick, or symbol. On a rare occasion, however, you will find an idea that demands *single minor character* viewpoint.

2. Single minor character

With this viewpoint, a single minor character relates the story about a major one. Various situations suggest a simple minor character viewpoint. The major character may know too much for suspense, cannot appear in all the scenes, or dies in the story. Perhaps the author plans to do a series. At times you may need a more colorful character for background interest. The major character may offer poor reader identification. A character who murders his sweetheart or who influences teenagers to steal and murder for him offers poor reader identification.

Minor characters come in three varieties: participating, bystander, or implied narrator. The *participating narrator* appears more often in stories. This narrator becomes involved in the major character's problem, makes the decision for action along with the major character, and shares in the character change and theme. Let's write from the viewpoint of another dealer, probably an older woman, as the participating narrator:

I promised Harriet I'd look out for Natalee, help her all I could with the antiques show. I soon realized she didn't need the help of an old woman but that of an eligible man with a good business head. So I set out to find one for her.

Establish immediately, as in the example, the sympathetic connection between the participating narrator and the major character, and imply that both will learn from the events of the story. You may or may not create the narrator and the major character of the same sex. Some authors think the same sex simplifies the writing.

The *bystander* merely reports the action of the character and colors the story with his emotional reporting. For this role, select a person who has daily contact with a variety of people. The owner of a bookstore might report the action of a young man and woman who met in his shop, or the postman might tell of the romance of two people on his route. Do not involve the bystander in the problem, the decisions, or the major character change. Of the three types of narrators, this one appears the rarest because of the low-key emotion and poor reader identification, as this example shows:

> The young man completed unloading the van when the girl arrived in a battered station wagon and headed for the same space. She climbed out of the car. "I'm afraid you have the wrong space." She handed him the registration card.
>
> "Not my mistake," he said and shook his head. He handed her his registration card. The office had already found the error, and the promoter came around the corner at a fast pace.

In recent years some writers have experimented with the *implied narrator*, an interesting variation of minor character viewpoint. The author assumes the role of the narrator in the story but never identifies himself with a personal pronoun; yet he provides the emotional coloring. Nonfiction writers have long used this type of viewpoint. Study this example:

> Anyone could see that Steve and Natalee belonged together. They loved antiques, came from the same background—educated, too. The romance might have blossomed right there at the antiques show if the other man had stayed out of Natalee's life.

With minor character viewpoint, you can cover a longer span of time than in the average short story. Beware of these three pitfalls: the author puts another person between the reader and the major character; frequently the minor character overshadows the major one; and the author narrates what takes place rather than shows the characters through conflict action and dialogue of a scene. We call this the viewpoint trap.

3. Dual viewpoint

Today, authors rarely choose *omniscient viewpoint*, which shares the thoughts of all the characters. With the limited wordage of the short story, you waste too many words transitioning smoothly from one character to the next. Shifting viewpoint in a short story can create too much confusion and difficulty for the reader to identify with any of the characters. Save multiple viewpoint for the novel or novelette.

In recent years, however, authors have experimented with *dual viewpoint* in short stories for women's magazines. With this viewpoint, the reader views the story through the eyes of two major characters who share the same problem and work toward a common solution. You may follow either the situation or the character trait pattern. Open with one character and show her problem. Transfer to the other character so he can relate his side of the problem.

Bring the two characters together in the complications, shifting back and forth between viewpoints. The crisis lets the two characters find the common solution, but use the viewpoint of the one who opened the story. Both characters contribute to the character change in the climax.

What if a young couple decided to get a divorce, but both want the dog? The viewpoint will shift back and forth between the husband and the wife, with each giving one side of the problem. The crisis brings them together when something happens to the dog. The climax reveals they have too much in common to get a divorce.

Dual viewpoint steals wordage from the action and characterization, splits the reader's sympathies, lessens suspense, and disrupts the continuity. You actually write two stories but get paid for only one. If you can develop your idea only with dual viewpoint, then go ahead and try it.

If you cannot decide on the best character for the viewpoint, try writing several paragraphs for each of the three major characters. Generally, the words flow rapidly when you find the best viewpoint character. A more accurate method of selecting the viewpoint consists of knowing the definite functions this character must perform.

Functions of the Viewpoint Character

While other characters may perform some of the following major functions, only the viewpoint character meets the specifications of all six. Since most published stories favor single major character viewpoint, we will concentrate on this type. See if your character can perform these functions:

1. Emotion

In all short stories the viewpoint character supplies the dominant emotion that evolves from the problem situation or character trait. We discuss character trait in the next chapter. The viewpoint character may want love, popularity, recognition, or the clarification of a mystery. The other characters, setting, immediacy, and gimmick-symbol reenforce this dominant emotion created by the viewpoint character. Natalee's involvement with the two men and the antiques setting provide romance, as in this example:

> When she finished the ham sandwich and coffee Steve took from an old picnic basket, he reached inside again for a tiny round cake and placed it before her on the table. The blur in her eyes almost dimmed the inscription: "Happy Antiquing."
>
> "I could kiss you," she whispered and squeezed his hand.
>
> "I have no objections," he said in a legal tone.
>
> Mrs. Devereaux peered over the partition at them. "Celebrating something?"
>
> Steve nodded. "A very special occasion."

Analyze the characters in your story treatment and select as the viewpoint character the one whose need will best supply the dominant emotion you wish to project to the reader.

2. Conflict

Conflict develops from the viewpoint character's struggle with his thoughts—inner conflict—and from the disagreements with the other characters—outer conflict. Screen your characters for the one with the most vital problem—vital to him—to solve, and with the character trait which stimulates forceful inner conflict and outer struggle with other characters. When these conflicts center around one certain character and affect his love, career, or way of life, make that character your viewpoint. In the following example Natalee explains her inner struggle to like or not like Steve:

> Natalee found Steve exasperating. He accused her of not wanting to sell the Tiffany vase because of its high price. He guessed the truth, but she didn't intend to admit it and let him gloat. But when she started to tell him off, he disarmed her with some little consideration, like talking a customer into buying the Heisey pitcher no one seemed to want at a bargain price. He raised the price and sold it. But thinking about it made her angry she hadn't known to raise the price herself.

This dialogue shows the outer conflict between Natalee and Kenneth:

> Natalee looked up surprised to see Kenneth suddenly appear at the booth in the antiques show.
>
> "We've got it made," he said. "Mrs. Crandall wants the Larkins' stuff."
>
> Natalee didn't experience the elation she expected. "So the Larkins got the job of decorating." Kenneth shook his head.
>
> "Not exactly. It's up to you," he confided, and lowered his voice as Steve appeared. "Mrs. Crandall wants you to authenticate the junk. I told her to bring it here."
>
> Natalee grew more confused. "So how does that affect me?"
>
> Kenneth looked disgusted. "Tell her it's the real stuff. The Larkins buy; we buy the partnership." He flashed her the old achievement smile.
>
> "But what if the antiques are—" She never completed

the protest for the Crandalls hurried toward them lugging a box.

Natalee will encounter no trouble carrying both the inner and outer conflict of the story.

3. Suspense

Suspense develops from the viewpoint character's continued efforts to solve the problem created by the opening situation. Consequently this character must appear in all the scenes, vacillating between the right and wrong decision. In trying to solve the problem, she knows the least about the other characters' motives.

If your character knows too much, you fall into the trap of withholding facts from the reader for suspense. At the end of the story, the reader experiences a letdown, since you cheated him, withholding known facts for a false suspense. Suspense builds, not from *will* the character solve the problem, but from *how* the character works out the situation.

Suspense builds in our example story from a number of complications. Will Natalee sell the business? Will she make a success of the show? Will she fall in love with Steve? Will she marry Kenneth? Will she help the Larkins? Will she help the Crandalls? How will she discover the right man for her?

4. Reader identification

For the viewpoint character, select the one with whom the reader identifies the quickest and most substantially. In this way the reader becomes the character and experiences the action of the story. Create a viewpoint character similar to the reader of the magazine you hope to sell. The character may have a similar background, a familiar problem, or conflict with characters the reader knows.

The reader of a magazine aimed at homemakers will identify with a character wanting recognition from her family, the reader of an adventure magazine with a marathon runner or a hunter stalking game.

In the Natalee story, the reader will identify with the romance, the antiques, and the show background.

5. *Author's message*

Every story, through its viewpoint character, leaves the reader with some worthwhile thought or theme— the author's message. In the climax, you summarize in a brief statement what the major character has learned from the story action.

If your material demands a participating narrator, then this character states the message. With dual viewpoint, each character must contribute equally to the theme. Naturally, single major character viewpoint assures the most convincing and well-remembered message for the reader.

Select as your viewpoint character the one who has the most to win or lose by the outcome of the story action and the one who provides the most believable possibility for change. The change in the character does not mean a total overhaul of a bad personality but merely bringing one negative facet or blind side of a basically good personality into positive focus. Avoid the impossible of trying to change an all-bad character into an all-good one. Projecting a positive message means moving from weakness to strength in the viewpoint character. The next chapter discusses in detail the degree of character change in relation to the type of character trait.

Here Natalee sums up her character change and the theme:

> Natalee looked at the reproduction beside the Tiffany vase. Even Kenneth saw the glaring difference and

stormed away. Steve grinned and slipped an arm around her. It felt very right. Sometimes you must listen to your heart instead of your head.

6. Ability

A story consists of a problem which the major character must solve. The character must possess the ability, physical set up, or experience to *make decisions and act on them*. The participating narrator shares this function with the major character. (Mention this for any character early in the story.)

Natalee has grown up working with antiques. She has the ability to recognize fakes or reproductions.

Stop right here and give the major character in your story the above six-point test. Choose the character who best performs all functions. When you know your viewpoint character, you want to think of ways to project him to the reader.

Six Ways to Show Your Viewpoint

To sell you must show the characters in action, for writing means *show* business. You, the author, furnish both the audio and the video with your words. The reader believes only what you *show* him. He will challenge or skip over anything you *tell* him. With the following devices you can show or project the viewpoint character:

1. Action

How the viewpoint character acts reveals his true self. Action without conflict between characters reads flat and pointless, so put your character under stress to make decisions. To increase the emotional conflict, interweave some thoughts of the viewpoint character.

In this example the author narrates rather than shows:

Natalee took the wrapping from the Tiffany vase and put it on the display shelf. She rested a moment before she removed the tissue from another item. Steve looked at the vase. Natalee waited impatiently for his comment.

We wrote the facts, but we did very little projection. Let's show the same facts with emotion:

Natalee removed the soft tissue from the small Tiffany vase with the greatest care and placed it safely in the center of the display shelf. For a second she stood and admired it. Steve picked it up and looked at the price. "You priced it so it wouldn't sell." He replaced it and went back to unpacking. She resented his reading her thoughts, almost the way Aunt Harriet used to do.

2. Dialogue

Dialogue makes characters come alive for the reader. Since the full discussion of dialogue comes in Chapter 7, let's continue the previous example:

"It's worth every penny of that," she challenged and reached for the next item.

"If you say so," he said and placed a lacy old valentine by the vase.

She shouldn't have agreed to share the booth. Kenneth wouldn't like it. Steve looked thoughtful.

"I fall in love with things, too, and can't bear to sell them, like this old valentine," he admitted.

"So what if I do want to keep it," she muttered. He chuckled.

Each line of dialogue must characterize and develop the story action. Certainly the dialogue must conform to your picture of the viewpoint character; otherwise you must explain in his thoughts why it doesn't.

3. Thoughts

The viewpoint character carefully confides his thoughts and reactions to the reader. If he says one thing and does another, he must tell the reader why. Thoughts form the hotline to the reader, so the reader must see the viewpoint character weigh the decisions, react to the other characters, and argue the right or wrong choice of action, keeping the inner conflict rising. Never let your viewpoint character withhold facts from the reader to give a surprise ending. The reader will not trust you again. In this example Natalee shares her thoughts:

> Natalee took an instant dislike to Mrs. Larkin. She could find no real reason for her feelings. She guessed she disliked Mrs. Larkin because she acted so condescendingly about buying the antiques.

Remember to write the viewpoint character's thoughts in the same style as the dialogue and with the same personal pronoun.

To learn how to write thoughts, take a well-written story from a current magazine and underline the thoughts with a red pencil. Mark the dialogue in green. Now study the proportions of the two.

4. Reactions of supporting characters

You can project the major character through the actions and reactions of the other characters, as in this example:

> Natalee stepped right out of the car into Steve's arms. She put her head on his shoulder and sobbed. He smoothed her hair and tightened the hold. She clung to him until the tears stopped, then she pulled abruptly away.

This example shows a dependent Natalee who needs Steve's strength.

5. Author's statement

Any time you, the author, step in and take the story from the viewpoint character, you interrupt reader identification. On a rare occasion, you can sandwich a line of description between the thoughts or the dialogue of the major character, or open a story with an author's statement and then shift to major character viewpoint. The editor may not notice these slight interruptions, but he will if the author takes over the story continually.

6. Other devices

The amateur will try to get across information by quoting an advertisement, a letter, or even a diary. Thus:

> Natalee read Steve's card: Cow Palace Antiques Show, Row C, Space 50, Building Annex. Her space card also read Row C, Space 50.

The professional writer makes sure the major character tells the reader the content, but then he moves on with the action, as these details only clutter the story. Write them this way:

> Natalee took Steve's assignment card and compared it to hers. Someone had given them the identical assignment!

Avoid documentary projection, since you mark yourself as a lazy and unimaginative amateur.

A telephone conversation where you report only one side, thinking you add suspense, fails utterly in projecting the character. Consider this example:

> When Natalee realized she couldn't get set up in time to meet Kenneth, she telephoned him.
> "I can't get there until nine," she said.

"But I can't set up in the morning," she argued.

"Well, maybe I can work out something. I'll get there on time," she said and hung up.

The professional writer develops both sides of the conversation along with the viewpoint character's reactions to the caller. This treatment makes the telephone conversation appear as an action scene, as in this example:

When Natalee realized she couldn't get set up in time to meet Kenneth, she telephoned him.

"I can't get home until nine," she said. He said nothing for a long moment.

"Finish setting up in the morning," he said bluntly. She wouldn't have time before the show opened.

"I can't," she argued, and hoped he would understand.

"I can't reach the Larkins this late. Forget the show." He sounded so angry she backed down.

"Well, maybe I can work out something," she agreed, and hung up.

You also can project the viewpoint character through figures of speech and sensory impressions—techniques discussed in the next chapter.

Editors and readers prefer single major character viewpoint, so we will concentrate on that. From now on we will refer to this character as the *Viewpoint*.

Your time has come to work. Choose the Viewpoint and write several paragraphs using each of the above types of projection. To complete the projections, however, you must learn the various devices for developing character.

Projecting Believable Characters

A salable short story must have forceful and lifelike characters. To create vivid characterization, the supporting characters should intensify the inner conflict of the Viewpoint by helping or hindering the solution of the problem. The Viewpoint reacts by trying to win acceptance from the other characters. Thus the problem and the character trait you choose for the Viewpoint furnishes the key to the inner and outer conflict in the story. The problem puts him in conflict with the other characters, and the negative and positive facets of the trait create the inner conflict.

The Single-trait Viewpoint

A *trait* in a short story differs considerably from the common meaning of "trait" as a distinguishing characteristic we see in people around us. In real life, people rarely change, or they change very slowly. In a short story, however, the major character must change in the course of the story from the way you presented him at the beginning. Thus a trait in a short story normally means a temporary condition that can change—not an inveterate feature of someone's personality. The trait itself determines whether you need a superficial or an in-depth change.

Since the Viewpoint in a short story has only one trait, we call this a *flat* characterization. In a novel, by comparison, you develop *round* characterization by giving the Viewpoint at least *three* traits. To give a flat character the illusion of roundness, you alternate between the negative and the positive facet of the trait, overlay with at least two tags and motivate with incidents from the past. A *tag*, discussed in detail below, shows the outer person, while a trait focuses on the inner one.

Natalee, for instance, decides one minute she will sell the antiques business, and then the next minute wonders why she ever considered the idea. The sudden death of the aunt on whom she depended motivates this trait of indecisiveness. A mental tag shows her sentimental about old Tiffany, and the name tag— Natalee— implies, in my opinion, a feminine woman. The two tags project an illusion of roundness for Natalee's flat trait.

Remember that at the opening of the story the negative facet dominates the Viewpoint to create the problem, but at the solution the positive facet takes command to solve the problem happily. The amount of change in the Viewpoint depends upon the type of trait you choose.

1. *Image trait*

When you think of a situation pattern, you devise a Viewpoint to carry the action. The faster you project the Viewpoint to the reader, the sooner you can begin the action. An *image trait* stimulates quick reader identification with very few words.

The reader must quickly recognize the image upon which you base the trait. When you mention the familiar image, the reader fills in the associated details. Certain words conjure up general images: rube, southern belle, granny, ivy league, football player, professor, or judge. You may give the character the image of a movie star, a politician, or a high-powered salesman. The divorced father who wants to make visiting day perfect has an image trait, but it does not fit the Natalee story.

You need not restrict yourself to general images. A comparison of your Viewpoint with a well-known personality in the public eye proves very effective. The pages of history also offer good image traits. Once you establish the image, your reader supplies the background, physical appearances, and other necessary details for the complete picture.

A reverse play on the accepted image lends freshness. A librarian hates to read books, or a politician refuses to make any campaign promises.

You can create two other reversals. Let the character picture himself in the wrong image and try to live up to it. A man sees himself as a playboy and discovers he wants to love only one woman. In another example, the Viewpoint tries to hide the true image but eventually reveals the correct one. A woman tries to hide her intelligence to get a man, only to reveal it when he needs a solution to a pressing problem.

With the image trait, the character changes very slightly in a short-short or in a story that emphasizes situation. The Viewpoint corrects the wrong image, consequently the trait requires little motivation.

2. Human trait

While the image trait depends on the reader's quick conjuring up of a general mental picture, the *human trait* emphasizes an excusable weakness or imperfection, such as procrastination or laziness. Everyone knows the person who plans to go on a diet next week, promises to do a job tomorrow, or can't say "no" to a request for help. These human frailties not only endear a Viewpoint to the reader, they also offer quick reader identification. The reader either has the trait or knows someone who does.

The type of human trait you select can actually influence the sale of the story. Always choose a trait which will draw a chuckle, not a frown of disapproval from the reader—or select a trait easily excused as "only human." People usually admire genuine curiosity, for example, but frown on malicious, damaging gossip.

Give the Viewpoint an "only human" trait when you choose the situation, slice-of-life, or circle pattern. Since the Viewpoint changes merely to recognize his weakness, you need only enough flashback to establish the trait. Flashback covers the life of a character during the time before the opening of the story.

3. Self-discovery trait

The *self-discovery trait* adapts to any pattern that emphasizes situation or the combination of trait and situation. This trait requires a stronger character change and theme than are necessary for the image or "only human" traits. Flashbacks must adequately explain the origin of the trait. But though it uses more flashback than the image or human traits do, it needs less than the other character traits.

The trait originates from a positive or negative source. While a character may have a positive trait, it becomes negative when he carries it to an extreme. Most people, as an example, consider saving for a rainy day a positive trait, but the person who never spends a dime for any pleasure becomes a miser.

So the Viewpont with the self-discovery trait starts

the story excessively positive—too romantic, too irresponsible, or too impulsive. During the action of the story, the Viewpoint gradually changes to find a happy balance between the two excesses.

If you work from the negative source, the Viewpoint at the opening of the story has a very low opinion of her ability and discovers in the crisis a new and stronger facet of personality. Natalee, for instance, must waiver indecisively over selling the business, the right man to love, or identifying a reproduction. At the crisis she changes from indecisive to decisive.

4. Mistaken-idea Trait

The mistaken-idea trait creates the action in the character pattern. The Viewpoint starts out believing one thing and gradually corrects the mistaken idea. The Viewpoint in the religious, the women's, and especially the confession magazines has this trait. Since a situation in the past motivates the trait, you will need a flashback to explain the origin of the trait to the reader. A flashback also keeps the Viewpoint sympathetic, no matter how negative the trait.

Do keep in mind that this trait evolved during a relatively short period of time before the story opened. The shorter the time, the slighter the character change. But regardless of the amount of Viewpoint change, you will need a strong theme.

The woman whose son lost sight in one eye has a mistaken-idea trait. She feels that the boy who caused the accident must pay for his carelessness. A short flashback reveals she has poor eyesight and nearly went blind because of a childhood accident. She eventually learns that revenge only causes more tragedy.

5. Wrong-attitude trait

The *wrong-attitude trait* differs from the mistaken-idea in that it grew over a long period of time and embitters the Viewpoint. A flashback shows how the trait came about so that the reader will sympathize with or understand the Viewpoint.

The trait requires the character pattern in which the Viewpoint finally recognizes he has the wrong attitude and should change. The amount of change depends on how negative you make the attitude. In the confessions, never show a complete change but let the major character work toward changing day by day. The Viewpoint in the literary or quality story may recognize his wrong attitude too late for an upbeat ending.

Suppose a man feels that he can trust no woman. He developed this wrong attitude when his mother ran away with another man. His father continually warned him, "You can never trust a woman." His wrong attitude costs him the woman he loved. The market will determine the ending.

6. Flaw

The greatest Viewpoint change comes with a *flaw*. A flaw includes an unethical trait, such as lying, cheating, stealing, or killing. The Viewpoint changes and tries to atone—never use a miraculous cure. For understanding, the trait needs forceful motivation with a flashback. Even then the reader will see him as someone else and will not identify. A character emphasis or biter-bit story uses the flaw trait. A Viewpoint in a confession story, along with lesser "sins," may show a flaw.

The religious and women's magazines prefer a sympathetic minor character as the Viewpoint for reader identification. The men's and quality markets do not soften the flaw but let the Viewpoint become more negative. The alien who let his cheapness trap him has a flaw. New writers should avoid this trait until they have more experience in writing.

7. Distinctive trait

The *distinctive trait* places the Viewpoint in a category by himself with a specialized ability. He may exhibit the power to foresee the future or to solve murder cases by mathematical deductions. While this trait works well with any type of story, you find it more with science fiction, detective, or fantasy.

The character may remain the same and face more problems because of his gift, may lose his unique ability, or may decide never to use it again. Your problem consists of making the trait believable. Plausibility comes with showing the trait in action, again and again, so the reader accepts it.

Only three characters in a story have a trait: the Viewpoint, and the positive and negative supporting characters. Natalee shows indecision about selling the business. The traits of the supporting characters must overlay the negative and positive facets in the Viewpoint's trait. Steve, a reliable person, tries to stop Natalee from selling. Kenneth tries to manipulate her to sell so he can buy a real-estate partnership.

The supporting characters do not change but keep the same trait throughout the story. The change comes in the Viewpoint, who sees the characters one way at the beginning of the story and in their true light at the end.

Functions of the Supporting Characters

Supporting characters never wander aimlessly through a story; they must perform a specific function.

1. Positive supporting character

From the opening of the story, the positive supporting character, whether a man or a woman, tries to help the Viewpoint with the right solution to the problem. As a result, you open the story with the Viewpoint in conflict with this character. If the positive supporting character, through the complications, succeeds in influencing the Viewpoint to make the right decision, the story ends happily. The reverse happens if he fails.

In the single viewpoint story, the trait of the supporting character remains the same throughout the story. In a rare exception, if the story deals with a teenager and a parent, or with a young married couple, well-established authors sometimes imply a slight change in the trait of the positive supporting character. These writers have learned how to accomplish this deftly, without stealing from the Viewpoint's change. Know your craft thoroughly before you try it.

In the dual viewpoint story, the two major characters act as positive supporting characters for each other. With minor character viewpoint, the major character and the participating narrator share the positive supporting character.

With dual or single major character viewpoint, the positive character appears immediately in the problem situation with the Viewpoint. When the story has a participating narrator, this supporting character appears after you establish the relationship between the Viewpoint and the major character.

Steve Atkins serves as the positive supporting character in the Natalee story.

2. Negative supporting character

The negative supporting character influences the Viewpoint to stay on the wrong course. The Viewpoint starts the story in agreement with this negative character but changes at the moment of revelation. Establish the negative supporting character along with the positive one. If you can't bring him in at the beginning of the story, get him firmly in the Viewpoint's thoughts or in a conversation of the characters in the opening problem situation. Most emphatically, place him in the crisis scene with the Viewpoint and the positive supporting character for the moment of revelation. By all means give to the negative character the same amount of time with the Viewpoint as you give to the positive character.

Kenneth plays the role of the negative supporting character.

3. Minor motivating characters

Most stories contain minor characters who assist the supporting characters and intensify the conflict for the Viewpoint. Introduce these characters in the problem situation by bringing them on scene, referring to them in conversation, or implying their role through their profession.

We mention other dealers setting up and Natalee dreading to meet her aunt's old friends. In this way, at the outset of the story we imply the dealer Mrs. Devereaux through her profession, even though she does not appear until later in the story.

The number of minor characters depends upon the strength of the Viewpoint's problem, the trait, the amount of change, and the motivation. *Motivation* tells why the characters behave the way they do. The minor characters create the minor conflict which feeds the dominant one.

Learn to use couples to double the value of minor characters: The Larkins support the wrong decision, and the Crandalls the right one.

4. Theme character

A theme character does not appear in every story. He functions as a minor character and points out both sides of the situation for the Viewpoint, so as to emphasize the balance in the complication. To get the reader to accept this character as unbiased, make him a family doctor, a minister, or some other person of trust. He may also function both as a minor motivating character and as a theme character, particularly in a confession.

The Natalee story does not require a theme character, since the Viewpoint performs this function.

5. Background character

Not every story needs a special background character. Such a character personifies the era and the setting of the story. Often the minor character viewpoint functions as a background character, too. Practically any character may perform this function in the average story. If you emphasize setting as essential to the conflict, a background character can intensify the emotional conflict.

Mrs. Devereaux, an old-fashioned antiques dealer, functions as a background character.

6. Scene properties

Some stories require certain people on scene to complete the setting or to perform minor duties for realism. Since these people appear only as scene properties, do not elevate them to minor character function by naming them. Too much prominence misleads the reader, who expects such characters to reappear later in the story. Identify these walk-ons by occupation or service. Let them strut and fret their minutes but disappear nameless.

At the antiques show we use the check-in woman and the promoter as scene properties.

Keep your characters to a minimum in a short story. Learn the device of employing one character to serve two functions. Mrs. Devereaux serves both as a background and as a positive motivating character.

Characters Need the Means to Act

Endow all supporting characters with the ability to perform their specific functions. Steve makes shows, knows antiques, and practices law. Kenneth, a top real-estate salesman, has all kinds of contacts through his work. He met the Larkins and Crandalls through his job. The Larkins have a reputation as expensive decorators. The Crandalls, who have inherited money and own a Victorian house, can afford the Larkins.

In addition to talent and ability, provide the characters with the physical setup that enables them to perform their functions in the story. Such backgrounds make the story believable.

Steve brings collectibles to the show in his new van. Natalee owns a Victorian house and the antiques Kenneth wants to sell so as to invest in a real estate partnership. The Larkins own a decorating shop. The Crandalls have the house that needs decorating. Mrs. Devereaux occupies the exhibit next to Steve and Natalee.

1. *Tags make flat characters round*

Think of character tags as visual devices that give the reader quick and explicit recognition of a character. They make the Viewpoint and the supporting characters appear round and give the illusion of a trait to the minor characters. The function of the character determines the number of tags.

Tags can project a character as negative or positive. A negative tag includes a snide manner, a raucous laugh, or yellow stained teeth. By contrast, a positive tag could include a generous mouth, a firm handshake, or an exotic aroma.

Giving a supporting character a positive trait and a strong negative tag makes the Viewpoint see only the outer person or the wrong picture. The other supporting character has a negative trait and a strong positive tag, so the Viewpoint focuses on the visual.

Make no character all black or all white, but rather a little of both. In summary, a strong negative tag can hide a positive trait, or a forceful positive tag can disguise a negative character.

To make a tag effective, you need to spotlight it at least three times before the reader remembers it. You need not use the same wording to show the tag, but do give the same picture. Mrs. Devereaux wears her gray hair in an upswept style. Toward the end of the day Natalee notices that a strand of gray hair hangs limply from Mrs. Devereaux's otherwise immaculate hairdo; and on the last day Mrs. Devereaux quickly sprays her gray hair to keep it in place.

A complete physical description of a character, a slang phrase in a one-time speech, or a single act do not make a tag. Only through repetition can a tag project the character without mentioning the name.

1. Name tag

This tag depends upon the general connotation of a name. The names of Beauregard or Mary Lou kindle an association with the South. Maria and Jose could project a character of Spanish descent. Nicknames especially describe a character: Fatso, Beefy, Red, Shorty, Slim, or Baldy. The names of young characters often end in y, like Jimmy, Patty, Andy, or Janey. Many readers associate the names of Dave, John, Catherine, or Martha with a "good" person. Jonathan, Hattie, and Maggie have an old-fashioned ring.

Connotations of names, however, change from generation to generation and from region to region, so make sure that the potential reader shares your projection. Do not depend entirely on the general connotation of a name but reenforce it with other character devices. Try reversing the tag by giving a dainty woman a masculine name, or a brawny man a sissy name. Finally, test your own reaction and those of others to a name.

You'll find any number of sources for names: the telephone directory, name books, magazines, newspapers, school yearbooks, and suggestions from friends. Some dictionaries and books give certain meanings to particular names, and these definitions might suggest possible projections. A number of writers keep a card file on names that interest them. You might find this helpful, too.

To me, "Natalee" has a soft, feminine sound that suggests dependency. I hope that most readers will picture a "Steve" as reliable and a "Kenneth" as self-centered.

2. Action tag

Actions speak louder than words. Under this tag comes any movement of the body: a helpless little gesture, a quivering chin, a fluttering hand, a shrug of the shoulders, a shifting gaze, or knuckle popping. Some action tags might suggest strength: a direct stare, firm handshake, or squared shoulders. Make a habit of noticing people's actions and try to classify them as positive or negative tags.

Kenneth rattles the change in his pocket when he grows impatient. Steve has an infectious grin.

3. Speech tag

Speech tags can include a wide range of mannerisms. In the most common speech tag, a character constantly repeats a phrase, such as "no fooling" or "you know what I mean."

Kenneth always speaks most persuasively of "our future together" or continually begs Natalee to "do it for me, for us."

Inflection or tone of voice can tag a person. Some people deliver their words dramatically, no matter how unimportant, while others have a habit of letting the voice dwindle to a whisper. Your character may speak rapidly and run words together, or talk so slowly that others want to put words in his mouth.

A character may speak loudly, with a husky tone, mumble his words, or drawl. You describe the tone of voice or delivery following the spoken words.

So speech tags include words, tone of voice, and delivery.

Do avoid speech impediments, however, such as a lisp, that may sting rather than amuse. Such tags can alienate readers and editors.

Add dialects or attempts at dialects to the "no-no" category. These make the reader struggle to get the meaning.

4. *Background tag*

You can tag characters by occupation, age, education, geographical areas, organizations, social status, or religion, to name only a few.

We have tagged all our characters with background. Natalee deals in antiques, Steve practices law, Kenneth sells real estate, and the Larkins work as interior decorators—all tags of professions. We use the background tag for the Crandalls: a young married couple who come from wealthy families.

5. *Sensory tag*

The five senses offer an endless supply of tags, but concentrate on those rarely used. Writers have greatly overworked sight with such tags as flaming hair, clear blue eyes, turned-up nose. The other senses suggest exceptionally good tags: the aroma of lilacs after a rain, a lemony scent, or a freshly bathed smell. Imagine the touch of a lover's hand, the grip of a nervous woman, or the coldness of a farewell kiss. Consider such hearing tags as a cigarette cough, shallow breathing, or stealthy footsteps.

6. *Mental tag*

Characters, like real people, think in certain patterns. Mental tags can project weakness or strength. Some characters think slowly while others quickly compute.

Steve thinks logically, analyzing each situation. Natalee reveals a sentimental strain in her thoughts as she clings to the memory of the time when she and her aunt worked together. Kenneth thinks first of himself and what he wants, then devises the quickest way to accomplish the goal.

You show these mental tags through the dialogue and

action of all characters, and through the reactions of the Viewpoint.

7. Figures of speech

You can project your characters with figures of speech. In writing for young readers with limited experiences, figures of speech provide quick and clear pictures. Mature readers demand cleverness in well-turned phrases or chuckle material.

Figures of speech can individualize a character, create a mood, or visually depict a setting. Too many figures of speech, as well as the trite ones—eyes as blue as the sea, hair black as the raven, action as quick as a wink—can overload the emotion and black out the story line.

These examples show the possibilities for figures of speech in characterization:

A *simile* compares one thing to another: "Natalee thought the antiques show glittered like a carnival she remembered as a little girl."

A *metaphor* substitutes one thing for another: "When you sell the business, you kill the goose that lays the golden egg," Steve said.

Personification endows the inanimate with human powers: "The Tiffany vase reached out to Natalee."

Irony says one thing but means another: "So you have only my interest at heart," she accused Kenneth.

Metonymy lets one part stand for another: "The office caught the mistake and came to straighten out the matter."

Hyperbole deliberately exaggerates for emphasis: "You're the girl I intend to love for the next million years," Kenneth assured.

Paradox makes a contradiction: "Natalee learned a long time ago that sometimes you must lose to win."

To summarize, tags, including figures of speech, serve as labels on characters for quick recognition or as visible signs of a trait. Choose tags to complement, supplement, or contrast with a trait or another tag, but show them at least three times.

Put the names of each character in your story on a separate sheet of paper. First decide the negative and positive trait of the major character and choose the tags. Indicate the character change. Next take one character at a time and work out the trait, tags, ability, and function. Now you have a composite picture of each character.

Projecting Your Supporting Characters

Single major character Viewpoint prohibits you from entering the mind of any supporting character to reveal his thoughts. Neither do you stop the action as the author in order to surmise what the character thinks, to give background information, or to describe him. Three professional devices help you project the supporting characters:

1. Character action

The more you show your character in action with the Viewpoint, the clearer you project the function of the character:

Natalee opened the back of the station wagon to remove a box. Steve gently moved her aside and carried the carton to the display table. He motioned for her to start unpacking and headed for more antiques in the car. She watched him for a moment before she turned to the tissue-wrapped vase at the top of the box. How very nice not to lug the cartons from the car. He seemed a completely different man now they had settled their trouble over the space.

This example shows supporting character Steve and his actions toward Viewpoint Natalee. The reader wants Natalee to like him and forget Kenneth.

2. Dialogue

A full discussion of dialogue comes in Chapter 7, but let's write a short example which shows how to use dialogue to project a supporting character, Kenneth:

> She glanced up to see Kenneth hurrying toward her. "Remember the firm I mentioned. Well, they contacted me about buying a partnership," he began.
>
> "That's wonderful," she said, and wondered what brought him away from his job.
>
> "It is and it isn't. I didn't expect it to happen this soon. I don't have the money to swing the deal." He faced her squarely so he could look into her eyes.
>
> "You want me to sell some of the antiques?" She caught on fast.
>
> "The Larkins are interested and will come by tonight to see them," he added.

In this example, Kenneth relates in dialogue that he needs money to buy the partnership and has made an appointment with a couple to buy Natalee's antiques. This dialogue shows Kenneth manipulating Natalee, emphasizing his self-centered trait.

3. Reaction of the viewpoint character

Viewpoint reaction represents one of the best devices for projecting supporting characters, as in this example:

> Natalee took the small vase from Mrs. Crandall and carefully examined its iridescent glow, much too glaring for old Tiffany. Steve reached for the vase, but she ignored his outstretched hand and tightened her grasp. She didn't need to look at him to know what he thought. Kenneth stepped between Natalee and the Crandalls. His look sent the message, loud and clear.

To breathe life into your characters, do several projection paragraphs on each supporting character. When you can clearly picture your characters, then you decide what makes them act the way you depict them.

Motives Shape Your Characters

Motivation helps define the functions of the characters. It cues the reader to cheer for some characters and to hiss at others.

Viewpoint motivation shows the reader why the major character thinks and acts the way he does. *Supporting-character motivation* explains why each supporting character will either help or hinder the Viewpoint in the solution of the problem. With this double motivation, you urge the reader to climb inside the Viewpoint and share the story action. Hence motivation stimulates the reader to react in a predetermined manner toward the Viewpoint and the other characters.

Helping the Reader Identify

To select the correct motivation, look at your character's trait and situation to determine how the reader will react toward the Viewpoint. Once you know this reaction, estimate when the reader will identify. If you have a delayed identification, select motivating devices to influence the reader to identify with the Viewpoint sooner:

1. Self-identification or escape

For quick identification, give the Viewpoint some point in common with the reader, such as trait, problem, or background.

Traits like the following offer immediate self-identification: a recognizable type, like a young mother; a human frailty, like putting off going on a diet; or self-discovery, like finding out you have acted too impulsively. Occasionally the reader may identify with a (mistaken-idea) generalization, such as the belief that all wealthy people act self-centered.

Since the reader identifies sooner with situation than with character trait, for quick reader identification choose the type of story that emphasizes plot. Manipulate the devices of the story to produce a problem which parallels one in the reader's life. Any reader daily faces problems in love, money, career, health, or family relations. Place the action in a familiar setting: a home, neighborhood, well-visited city, or a small town. If you use a gimmick or symbol, select something within the reader's experience or understanding. Make the Viewpoint change and theme appropriate to the reader's life.

The actions of the supporting character likewise influence the reader to identify with the Viewpoint. If bad characters wrong the Viewpoint, the reader defends. When good characters stand up for the Viewpoint, the reader approves. Choose your supporting characters from people the reader sees every day and label them as friends or enemies. Normal reasons for liking or disliking the Viewpoint prove better than unusual ones.

Some readers wish to escape their true identity. The overworked mother escapes into the life of the glamorous career woman, and the shy bookkeeper becomes an astronaut.

In motivating for escape, employ the same devices as for self-identification and in exactly the same manner, with one exception—the glamorous or exotic setting supplies the escape element. Make the background details so enticing the reader will want to become a part of it. In the science fiction story, strive to make the fictional background plausible.

Reader identification for escape requires very little flashback. Interweave, as needed, any essential facts from the past into the forward action of the story. Flashbacks merely clarify the built-in, motivating devices of the story.

If you offer the reader every opportunity for self-identification or escape, he becomes the Viewpoint by the time you establish the setting, the problem, and the other two characters. With these devices, and with flashbacks for clarity, the reader steps inside the Viewpoint by the first few paragraphs.

The Natalee story offers the reader romance for self-identification and the world of antiques for escape. Since almost everyone has experienced some type of mix-up, consequently the reader identifies with Natalee as soon as she discovers the mistake in space assignments; and a flashback tells of her aunt's death. Some stories, however, require stronger motivation for reader identification.

2. Reader sympathy or plausibility

To motivate sympathy or plausibility for any trait, begin by intensifying the built-in devices. The setting must intensify the inner conflict of the Viewpoint, the symbol must show a tender side of him, and the supporting and minor characters must become types that would upset anyone. Increase the amount of inner conflict so that the Viewpoint shares more thoughts with the reader, and intensify the outer struggle with stronger supporting characters.

To reenforce these devices, introduce a series of incidents at the beginning of the story or a flashback before the first decision to motivate the development of sympathy or plausibility for the Viewpoint. The choice of the device and the length depend entirely on the character trait.

In a story that combines situation and trait, such as self-discovery, open with three incidents that show the combination rather than with a flashback. A woman, for example, gets imposed upon by her beauty operator, the other room mother at the school, and even her husband, so she decides to assert herself. When a strong self-discovery trait, such as being overly efficient, creates the action in a character story, a short flashback directly before the first decision showing the development of the trait makes the reader care.

The distinctive trait requires motivation for plausibility so that the reader will believe in the Viewpoint. Your material and the market should indicate whether you use three incidents at the beginning or a short flashback before the first decision to show how the Viewpoint became aware of his unusual power.

When the Viewpoint shows a strong mistaken-idea trait, such as feeling that the positive supporting character does not approve of her, you need a short flashback to show what caused the belief to develop. The stronger the mistaken idea, the more dramatically you write the flashback.

A slightly longer flashback will secure sympathy for a Viewpoint with a wrong attitude that has developed over a long period of time or with a slight flaw, such as lying to make life appear more glamorous.

The type of motivating device determines when the reader will identify with the Viewpoint. If three incidents show the trait at the opening, identification will come immediately; for the other kinds of traits, identification does not come until after the flashback. The reader will not sympathize with the mother who wants revenge until a flashback shows she has very poor eyesight and almost lost it because of an accident in her childhood.

The amount of character change depends entirely on the choice of trait. A Viewpoint with a wrong attitude or slight flaw changes more than one with a mistaken idea or a self-discovery trait. With a distinctive trait, the Viewpoint may either lose the power or decide not to use it again.

3. Reader understanding

The flaw and occasionally a strong wrong-attitude trait require motivation for understanding. A reader seldom merges with a Viewpoint who has a serious flaw. No one wants to identify with a liar or a murderer. But if you make the circumstances of the Viewpoint's past life so grim and unbearable that no one could have survived without moral deformity, the reader will at least understand why the Viewpoint acts and thinks the way he does.

In the biter-bit, however, the reader wants the Viewpoint to get caught and cheers when he does.

Motivation for understanding relies on all the devices for self-identity and sympathy, plus a long dramatic flashback which explains how the Viewpoint developed the flaw. From the Viewpoint's past, blow up dramatically one large segment or a series of powerfully related incidents which caused the flaw. As the story develops, the Viewpoint's thoughts and dialogue contain key words or phrases from the flashback to remind the reader of the past.

The flaw requires a character pattern. The inner

conflict of the Viewpoint increases with heavier motivation for the supporting characters. The change consists of the Viewpoint's agreeing to reform, and the theme carries a moral tone. Since such a change proves difficult to make plausible in the limited word length of a short story, merely imply that with time the Viewpoint will win this struggle to conquer his flaw.

Some of the men's markets imply the Viewpoint will eventually change. In the literary or quality story, a Viewpoint starts out with a flaw and gradually grows worse for the downbeat ending. Some women's magazines will substitute a sympathetic minor character as the Viewpoint to provide better understanding of an unsympathetic major character and thus improve reader identification. The minor character changes by understanding why the major one has the flaw and came to a violent end or now tries to reform. With this device the reader joins the narrator and analyzes the major character. Positive tags likewise offset the flaw.

Decide what reader reaction you want for your Viewpoint and develop the appropriate motivating devices for the supporting characters.

How to Motivate Supporting Characters

The motivating devices for the supporting characters indicate how they will influence the Viewpoint during the action of the story. At the beginning the Viewpoint usually distrusts the motives of the positive supporting character but at the end changes to see the error in judgment. The opening generally shows the Viewpoint trusting the motives of the negative supporting character and discovering the truth at the crisis. Frequently, motivating devices for these two characters may give one picture to the reader and the opposite one to the Viewpoint.

If the reader identifies strongly with the Viewpoint, you need less motivation for the supporting characters. With an unsympathetic Viewpoint, you increase the motivation for the supporting characters since they must exert a stronger influence.

The negative supporting character may have a positive trait, but his motivation makes it negative. Suppose you give the character the trait of ambition, but to achieve his goals he uses other people. So ambition in this case would become a negative trait. The kind of motivating devices for minor characters depends upon the importance of their role in the story.

1. Tags and traits

To motivate the supporting characters select a trait which intensifies the two facets of the Viewpoint's inner conflict. Kenneth, the manipulator, will urge Natalee to sell the business so he can move ahead in his career. Steve sees Natalee as a girl he wants to marry, but he knows the sale would leave too much of a void in her life. He thinks first of her.

For suspense and to avoid the all-white or all-black characterization, use tags to create doubts or show imperfections. Kenneth's positive tags of success in real estate and the way he speaks so confidently of "our future" whiten his negative trait of a manipulator to gray. Steve's negative tags of a financially uncertain young lawyer who has newly opened his own office and his blunt way of making Natalee face the truth blacken his strong trait of reliability, leaving him gray, too.

With the lesser supporting characters, tags point out motives. The Larkins must buy cheaply and sell dearly to keep the decorating business profitable. The Crandalls need to learn more about antiques to buy wisely.

Lonely Mrs. Devereaux looks for a stimulating interest in life, and Natalee and Steve fill the need.

2. Setting

The motivation of a character often comes from where he works or lives. The real estate partnership proves the motivating force in Kenneth's life. To win Natalee's trust and to stop the sale of her aunt's antiques, Steve realizes he has only the duration of the show. The purchase of the Victorian house influences the Crandalls to consult a decorator. The Larkins want to use Natalee's Victorian home to get the Crandall's decorating job. Mrs. Devereaux, who likes to play cupid, determines to get Steve and Natalee to fall in love before the show ends.

3. Gimmick-symbol

The gimmick-symbol shows a supporting or minor character's motivation. Any time a character becomes involved with a gimmick-symbol, you have implied motivation in the way each employs it. With the question of authenticity, the Tiffany vase—the gimmick—controls the fate of all the characters. If Natalee authenticates the vase, she will sell the business, invest in the real estate firm, and marry Kenneth. Calling the vase a reproduction means she will keep the business and most likely marry Steve. The Larkins lose the job, and the Crandalls turn to Natalee and Steve for help. Mrs. Devereaux must find another interest.

4. Action

What a supporting or minor character does reveals how he feels about a situation and the Viewpoint. Steve puts forth every effort to help Natalee set up the exhibit, sell her merchandise, and look after her car. Kenneth makes appointments without consulting her, urges her to sell the junk to help him buy a partnership, and influences the Crandalls to hire the Larkins. The Larkins act as if they do Natalee a favor with their condescending manner. The Crandalls hesitate to hire the Larkins out of distrust. Mrs. Devereaux continually tries to get Natalee to see the real Steve and fall in love.

5. Dialogue

What a supporting or minor character says may not agree with what he thinks or does. Kenneth constantly reminds Natalee, "You know my love for you always comes first." Yet he thinks first of the partnership and her assets.

Steve never says he feels attracted to Natalee, but he thinks of things he can do to make life easier for her, and he quickly suggests, "Let me take care of that for you."

On the other hand, what a supporting or minor character says can reveal his true motives.

The Larkins always compliment and then tear down, as, "It's lovely, but is that a chip on the edge? That would bring down the value." Mrs. Crandall speaks with the frankness of a child: "I love your home." Mrs. Devereaux constantly reminds Natalee, "Good men like Steve don't grow on trees."

6. Other characters

Characters motivate each other. Kenneth will find buyers for Natalee to get her to sell. Steve will do all he can to stop the sale. The Larkins will sit back and let others do the work and use pressure. Mrs. Devereaux constantly reminds Natalee about the good qualities of Steve, and him about the good qualities of Natalee.

The above six devices project the true motivation of the supporting and minor characters to the reader.

Determine the motivating devices for the characters in your story and write several paragraphs you can later incorporate in the first draft of the story.

Motivating with Scattered Flashback

A salable story always begins on the day of the problem, but the Viewpoint, of course, lived before that time. A *flashback* covers any event from the past life that motivates the Viewpoint's actions in the present. We have two types of flashback: *scattered* and *solid*. The Viewpoint's trait or the story situation determines the type of flashback you will want to use.

If the Viewpoint has an image or human trait in a situation story, the scattered flashback provides the necessary information from the past for the reader. When the Viewpoint has a self-discovery trait in a situation or situation-character story, scattered flashback will easily explain the information from the past.

To get the bits and pieces of flashback in at the correct spots, write the entire problem situation without flashback. List the facts your reader must know about the past in single sentences of dialogue or thoughts of the Viewpoint. Slowly read the story in the present. When you need a line of flashback to explain a reference or reaction, cut the paper with scissors and tape in the sentence. Continue to do this until you have worked in all the sentences, and the story of the past comes through clearly to the reader.

Let's write part of the opening of our example story to see how this method works for the scattered flashback:

Natalee Baxter parked the old station wagon near the entrance of the exhibition building and sat quietly for a moment to compose herself. If she could get through this antiques show, she might find the right answer to selling the business. She climbed out of the car and walked resolutely to the check-in desk to get her space number.

The woman looked over her glasses and then smiled. "Oh, Miss Baxter. *Welcome back. I'm sorry to hear about your aunt. My sympathies. She was a great gal.*" She dug through the file three times and finally found the card.

Natalee glanced at the number. "*This isn't the number you mailed me.*" She fumbled in her purse and pulled out the card.

The woman sighed deeply. "I know, but *yesterday afternoon they notified us we must use this annex instead of our regular building. So everyone has different spaces.* Yours is right by the first big door. Here's your tab for tables."

Minutes later Natalee parked by the big door and went inside to locate the space. A tall man began unloading cartons from a van at the large space with her number. "I'm afraid you made a mistake. This is my space," she said.

"Nope, it's mine," he said, and handed her his number. He grinned. "Looks like somebody goofed. I'm Steve Atkins."

She stood there trying to stop the world from whirling around her: *Aunt Harriet's sudden death, months of getting through probate court,* and now this mix-up.

The italicized words indicate the flashback. Note how they do not stop the story.

Motivating with Solid Flashback

As previously explained, a self-discovery or distinctive trait in a character emphasis story may use either a series of incidents at the opening or a flashback before the first decision to motivate the Viewpoint. If your Viewpoint has a mistaken idea, wrong attitude, or flaw, a solid flashback establishes motivation. This type of flashback comes immediately before the Viewpoint's first decision for action and may vary in length from three paragraphs to a page, depending on the trait.

The solid flashback contains all the information the reader needs to know to understand the story. Delete any additional flashback in any of the other parts of the story. Remind the reader of the solid flashback with key words or phrases in the Viewpoint's thoughts or dialogue.

Never go into solid flashback until you have established the Viewpoint's problem and trait, introduced the important supporting characters, and confronted the major character with a choice of action. The Viewpoint's past life influences his choice of action. The flashback leads into the past with a key word, the Viewpoint's trait, a question, a puzzling situation, a time period, or an emotional reaction. The device you choose to open the flashback must bring it back to the present.

We do not need a solid flashback for our story, but we will write one to see how various devices work. The men's magazines favor scattered flashback and as little of that as possible. They want nothing to interrupt the forward action. The solid flashback can stop the story and lose the reader with its tedious narration of facts. While the women's magazines and the confessions do favor some solid flashback, more and more they tend to shorten it. The majority prefer scattered flashback. You may write the solid flashback with a number of different devices:

1. A series of incidents

If you choose a self-discovery, a mistaken idea, slight wrong attitude, or distinctive trait, a series of incidents may take care of the solid flashback for sympathy or plausibility. These incidents show how the Viewpoint acquired any of these traits. At times, this device works with a slight flaw.

To write the series-of-incidents flashback, select the happenings you will include and give them a *binder sentence* stating the time and the problem. The flashback would come right when Natalee must leave to meet Kenneth, and Steve offers to set up the exhibit:

> The last six months of her life had brought nothing but trouble and heartache [*binder sentence*]. While she and Aunt Harriet packed up after the last show, she heard a gasp. She turned to see Aunt Harriet crumpled on the floor. She died before Natalee could get help from the hospital.
>
> A week later the bills began to pour in. But the bank that handled the will said she couldn't sell anything until after probate. This entailed an item-by-item inventory and a cancellation of all shows.
>
> Several weeks later the doorbell rang, and Kenneth Preston wanted to know if she planned to sell the house. She burst into tears. He took her out to dinner and urged her to sell. "I can help you find some buyers," he offered.
>
> In fact, she couldn't have lived through those months without his help. They sort of drifted into dating regularly. And now at her first show another man offered to help her set up the exhibit, share the space transition back to the present. Why not accept his help?

We bring the reader up to date as to what has happened to Natalee and then show her accepting Steve's help so she can meet Kenneth and the Larkins. Note that each incident begins with a time peg to show forward movement.

The *V-plot* story uses a special arrangement of flashback incidents in a sequence to motivate each decision of the Viewpoint until the moment of revelation in the crisis.

The problem situation forces the Viewpoint to make an immediate decision. She remembers an incident in her remote past that guides her in making the decision. At each decision point in the complications, the Viewpoint makes no choice without remembering a similar incident in the past. Each incident from the past moves the story chronologically closer to the present and the crisis where the story line of the past (the left side of the V) intersects that of the present (the right side of the V). The Viewpoint no longer can look to the past for help and must consider only the present that brings about a moment of revelation. In the climax the theme speaks for both story lines.

2. Emotional reminiscence

In this type of solid flashback, the Viewpoint thinks back emotionally over the past. The emotional reminiscence can motivate the self-discovery, slight mistaken idea, and distinctive trait. A *had* with the verb in the first sentence of the flashback keys the opening. Then the verb shifts to the active past, as in the series of incidents, and continues until the last line when *had* reappears to end the flashback.

In this example we show why Natalee became so indecisive:

> Natalee *had* expected life to go on as usual indefinitely, then Aunt Harriet died. The two of them knocked on doors of strangers, followed up leads friends gave them, and canvassed flea markets for antiques. They split the chores right down the middle. Aunt Harriet took care of paying the bills, and Natalee researched the articles they bought and displayed them attractively at shows. They traveled from one show to the next. So many times Aunt

Harriet would laugh and say, "It satisfies the gypsy in me." They laughed together about the funny incidents and cried a little over the sad ones. Alone, she must take care of everything; yet she *had* not really accepted Aunt Harriet's death. Perhaps she should listen to Kenneth and sell the business.

Thus we see Natalee thinking about her life before Aunt Harriet's death.

3. *Dramatic action*

Dramatic action projects the flashback event with action verbs and dynamic Viewpoint emotion in the same patterns as the emotional reminiscence. In this example, you motivate Natalee's indecisiveness over selling the business. The first sentence takes you back into the past; the last sentence brings you back to the present:

Natalee could recall that night in every detail. They *started packing* after the show. Aunt Harriet com-*plained* of indigestion but *laughed* about it. Then she *gasped* and *pitched forward*, *grabbing* at the table before she *crumpled* to the floor. Natalee *screamed* and *knelt* beside her. People *crowded* around. Someone *called* an ambulance. Natalee *wadded* the cover from the table to *form* a pillow for Aunt Harriet's head and *frantically rubbed* the purplish hands to *start the circulation. She still had not recovered* from that night. She must not make a hasty decision about selling the business.

Note the entry and exit; italics mark the action words.

4. *A scene*

At times only a flashback scene will win the reader to the Viewpoint's side. Even then the reader will not sympathize but only understand the wrong attitude or accept some types of distinctive traits. How dramatically you write the scene depends on the strength of the trait and the need for change. You enter and exit the same way as with the other types of solid flashbacks.

This example shows why Natalee thought she might sell the business:

> After Kenneth left the building, Natalee went back over the events leading up to the appointment with the Larkins. Kenneth had first mentioned the partnership about a month ago. They returned from an early movie, and Kenneth sank into Aunt Harriet's favorite chair.
>
> "I picked up a rumor today," he said. "A very important real estate firm may take in a partner."
>
> "How does that affect you?" she asked and went to plug in the coffee. He sprang up and followed her.
>
> "You mean how does that affect us?" he corrected. He took her in his arms. "We could get married and have financial security. That's what a partnership means."
>
> She put her head on his shoulder. How nice to never worry again about packing and unpacking antiques, restocking. Her thoughts magnified the disadvantages of selling antiques. She had never thought the partnership would come up so soon and force her to make a decision about selling.

So Natalee had filed the thought of selling away in her mind, but Kenneth and the partnership bring it sharply in focus. As you can see, the Natalee story does not need a solid flashback, but you want to learn all the devices and keep them handy. You never know when you will need a solid flashback.

Two other devices of solid flashback include author's statement and a document relating the facts. If you rely on these, you brand yourself an amateur writer. These poor devices stop the action of the story, and you can lose your reader and the editor.

The solid flashback always motivates for necessary sympathy or for in-depth understanding of the Viewpoint. Effective devices for motivation make the reader share the past, struggle in the present, and care about the future of the Viewpoint.

When you have developed the motivation for all of your characters and written examples of the best devices, you want to learn how to block out the scenes of your story.

Scenes—Conflicts and Encounters

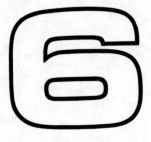

A story consists of a sequence of linking dramatic units called *scenes*. Scenes transform the story formula and the characterization into dramatic and purposeful forward action.

A scene differs from an incident or a happening in that it contains conflict between the Viewpoint and one or more of the supporting characters. A Viewpoint fighting two opposing forces within himself does not constitute a scene, but rather inner conflict. A Viewpoint fighting the forces of nature can constitute a special type of action scene.

If you plan your scenes according to a successful formula, your story will contain good continuity, forward movement, suspenseful action, and emotional conflict.

Blocking out the scenes before you write the story provides the means of combining your plot summary and your character development.

Elements of a Good Scene

Every scene contains certain basic elements. The combination of these essentials produces the formula. A scene formula helps you organize and integrate the action with the characters. Start with the *purpose*:

1. Purpose

Each scene should advance the story action by helping or hindering the Viewpoint in the solution of the problem. In one sentence, state the purpose of your scene. The opening scene confronts the Viewpoint with a problem and forces him to make a decision to take action. The complication scenes develop the conflict between the Viewpoint and the supporting characters, ending in a balance.

The crisis scene upsets the balance and pushes the Viewpoint to a moment of revelation. In the climax, the Viewpoint establishes his character change. Translate these general purposes into the specific action of your story. Knowing exactly why you need each scene guarantees unity and forward movement.

2. Time

A story takes place within a definite time period or immediacy. Each scene moves the Viewpoint nearer to the end of this time period and the solution of the problem. The first scene opens on the day of the problem in the Viewpoint's life. Establish the exact time of day as well as the length of time the Viewpoint has to solve the problem.

The complication scene may happen an hour later if your material demands. Allot the time from the first decision to establishment of the balance between the right and wrong efforts of the Viewpoint to solve the problem. Let the story material set the logical time for each complication scene to occur.

The crisis scene takes place immediately before the

end of the time limit. The climax occurs directly after the moment of revelation. Never have a gap of time between the crisis and the climax. From this general guide, determine specifically when each of your scenes takes place. The first line of each scene, as a rule, notifies the reader how much time has elapsed.

3. Place

No scene takes place in a vacuum. In a short story, restrict the settings to a few places by selecting a basic location, such as a community or home. With a home setting, scenes easily take place in the kitchen, living room, or patio. Avoid exhausting your reader by hopping from one new place to another, as from San Francisco to New York, New York to Paris, Los Angeles to Honolulu.

The problem situation opens in the basic setting, which you show between Viewpoint action and reaction. Never stop the action with long descriptive paragraphs of setting. The complication scenes move to a different area of the basic setting. For the crisis, try to return to the opening setting or one nearby. The climax continues in the same setting as the crisis.

Along with the new time, establish the setting at the opening of the new scene. Let the setting stimulate the inner and outer emotional conflict of the Viewpoint. Keep in mind that reader identification comes with familiar settings from everyday life. These settings require fewer words of description, for the reader fills in the details. With strange or exotic settings for escape identification, you must give far more details to get the reader to accept such backgrounds.

4. Characters

The Viewpoint appears in all scenes with one or more of the supporting and minor motivating characters to produce the conflict action. The Viewpoint's inner conflict determines which characters. Then you can equalize the negative and the positive decisions, establishing a balance for the crisis to upset.

In the problem situation, try to get the two supporting characters on scene. Who appears with the minor character Viewpoint depends on which type you choose. The participating narrator must establish the close relationship with the major character before you introduce the positive supporting character.

The character who appears with the Viewpoint in the complication scenes works toward setting up the balance between the positive and negative facets of the Viewpoint's trait. The same characters who appeared with the Viewpoint in the critical situation return for the crisis, but the climax needs only the Viewpoint and the positive supporting character for the happy ending.

5. Action

Three types of conflict action between characters can produce a scene: mental, physical, and emotional. In *mental* conflict the characters may reason, argue, or give information. With *emotional* conflict the characters beg, plead, persuade, or influence. *Physical* conflict includes slapping, walking away while the other person talks, or forcing a kiss.

To produce the scene conflict, one character becomes the aggressor. He may reason, threaten, or persuade the other character to take certain action. One character may beg while the other argues. The amount of conflict depends upon the location of the scene in the story sequence, the Viewpoint's trait or problem, and the importance of the opposing character.

The opening scene uses the mental conflict to give information and either one of the other two types of conflict. Never use more than two types. For the complication scenes, choose any two of the three conflicts which will best project your material. Keep the conflict in the last complication mild so as not to anticlimax the crisis, which employs all three types of conflicts. The climax scene gives information and ties up the loose ends.

Do keep in mind that you employ the type of conflict more than once. Show it in various degrees or shades of meaning. For example, a character may persuade, beg, sob, or storm, but all of these make up the emotional conflict. The exact shades of meaning provide unlimited possibilities for character conflict. In writing the summary of the action, try to choose words that indicate the type of conflict, such as: "He informed," "He persuaded," "He threatened," or "He warned."

6. Decision

The scene ends when the Viewpoint sums up his choices for action and chooses one as a possible way to solve the problem. Through thoughts or dialogue, share with the reader how the Viewpoint reaches this decision. Flashback, when necessary, motivates the decision in the opening scene and later by reference. This choice of action then involves the Viewpoint in a new difficulty which feeds the problem of the next scene.

To prepare the reader for this expanding problem, the Viewpoint confides the expected results, always stressing the happy solution and not thinking of the adverse possibilities. In the next scene, the Viewpoint finds himself in a worse situation than he could have imagined. In the complication scenes, the Viewpoint takes action which results in a balance between the negative and the positive decisions.

The crisis scene provides the Viewpoint with a moment of revelation where he sees the situation in focus and changes. Imply that he may lose all he wanted in the problem situation. He shows his change and earns the unexpected reward. This, with the theme, creates the upbeat ending.

The Natalee Story

Before we begin the scening for our model story, let's briefly picture each character. Natalee Baxter vacillates between selling and not selling the business—her problem. She changes from indecision to decisiveness.

Steve Atkins, a reliable person and struggling lawyer, thinks first of Natalee's happiness and urges her not to sell the business but instead to form a partnership with him.

Kenneth Preston, a successful realtor, wants to buy a partnership in a real estate firm, but he needs more money. He expects to get the money from the sale of Natalee's antiques business. He thinks first of his desires. Keep in mind that Kenneth has the inside track with Natalee at the opening of the story.

Scening the Natalee Story

To scene this story we will unite these characters with the plot action we summarized. Three factors determine the number of scenes: the time duration of the action, the strength of the Viewpoint's problem or trait, and the market requirements. The average story of twenty pages or 5,000 words requires approximately five to six scenes. We'll use five since the climax only continues the crisis.

Take five sheets of paper—one for each scene—and head each one with the appropriate scene number. Before you write a final version, do some shifting around of facts for better conflict. Try to do most of your revisions at this point before you write the story. When you have everything set, do the scene block-out:

1. Scene 1. Problem situation

Purpose: To introduce Steve and Natalee and let Kenneth put pressure on Natalee.

When: Friday afternoon.

Where: At antiques show.

Who: Natalee, Steve, Kenneth, Mrs. Devereaux, Larkins—all by name; check-in woman, show promoter.

What happens: Natalee Baxter chooses this antiques show, the first since her aunt's death, to determine if she should sell the business. She and Steve Atkins get assigned to the same space through a mix-up in changing exhibition buildings at the last minute. Since the space proves too large for either of them, and the promoter has no other, he offers to let them split the cost. Natalee can use this cheaper rate as she has not been able to sell any antiques because of probating her aunt's will. So she agrees, and Steve helps her unload and unpack.

When Steve goes to get a carton from her car, Kenneth Preston, her fiance, comes by to tell her he can buy a partnership in a real estate firm if he can raise the money. He has arranged for the Larkins, probable buyers, to look at her antiques that night. They can marry as soon as he buys the partnership. She introduces him to Steve, but Kenneth rushes off before she can explain about the mix-up.

Natalee unpacks a Tiffany vase, and Steve shows her a reproduction of it that he knowingly bought. Putting the two together shows the exceptional quality of the genuine vase, as Mrs. Devereaux from the next booth points out.

Natalee realizes she cannot complete the setup if she meets Kenneth and the Larkins on time. When she explains about an appointment with a buyer, Steve suggests he finish the job.

Decision: She accepts his offer.

2. *Scene 2. Complication 1*

Purpose: To involve Natalee in a plan to get the Crandall decorating job for the Larkins.

When: Friday night.

Where: At Natalee's Victorian home in San Francisco.

Who: Natalee, Kenneth, and the Larkins. The Crandalls by name.

What happens: Natalee has trouble starting the old station wagon. She barely arrives home before Kenneth. He confirms his love for her and puts their future in her hands. She tries to understand Kenneth's lack of appreciation for antiques.

The Larkins arrive and adopt a patronizing attitude as if they and not Natalee will make the decision about selling the antiques. Natalee dislikes them instantly and feels overjoyed when they say they do not have the money to buy at this time. Kenneth mentions the Crandalls, but Mrs. Larkin says they have not definitely made up their mind about the job even though she has taken them some of her finest antiques to consider. Kenneth suggests that they influence the Crandalls to buy by bringing the Crandalls to see Natalee's house and antique furnishings the next night. Natalee protests that she does not want this. Kenneth reminds her of their future. The Larkins say they will buy any antiques the Crandalls select. Kenneth voices his approval.

Decision: Natalee finally agrees to the proposal.

3. Scene 3. Complication 2

Purpose: To bring Steve and Natalee closer together.

When: Saturday.

Where: At the antiques show.

Who: Natalee, Steve, Mrs. Devereaux, customers.

What happens: Natalee, still upset over the Larkins, has trouble with the car. She gets more upset when she sees that Steve has mixed their antiques but used her shop sign, Heritage House Antiques, to make the exhibit look like a partnership. She consoles herself in that Kenneth will probably not come to the show and will not find out. Steve calms her with coffee and doughnuts, and she admits he created a beautiful exhibit. The customers think so, too. At lunch time he drags out a picnic basket with sandwiches and coffee. For dessert, he gives her a small cake inscribed "Happy Antiquing." Mrs. Devereaux wants to know the occasion. They offer her a piece of cake. She comments on what a perfect pair they make. By the time the show closes, they have sold so much that they both will need to bring more the next day. Steve mentions a partnership, but Natalee hesitates, not telling about the other situation. She plans to leave, but the car won't start. Steve offers to drive her home and to call a friend about fixing the car. He takes her in his arms, and she feels greatly attracted to him.

Decision: She accepts his offer to drive her home and get the car fixed.

4. *Scene 4. Complication 3*

Purpose: To force Natalee to bring the two men together.

When: Saturday evening.

Where: Natalee's home.

Who: Natalee, Steve, Kenneth, the Larkins, the Cran-dalls.

What happens: Steve and Natalee arrive late to find the others waiting. Steve insists on coming in to get the replacements for the show. Natalee remembers that she has not told Kenneth about Steve, but Steve explains all. The Larkins try to corner the Crandalls to keep them from Steve, but they have no luck. Steve and the Crandalls like each other, and he explains the values of the antiques and how to tell a reproduction. Kenneth blows up and tells Natalee to get rid of Steve. Natalee silently applauds the way Steve has cut the Larkins out of the picture, but she reminds Steve about the car. He goes in the kitchen with her to use the telephone and warns her that the Larkins and Kenneth plan to take advantage of her. He arranges about the car and says he will take her to the show the next day. Natalee can't stand any more feuding between Steve and Kenneth.

Decision: Natalee promises Steve she will delay selling anything to the Larkins.

5. *Scene 5. Crisis*

Purpose: To bring Steve and Natalee together.

When: Near closing time for the show.

Where: At the antiques show.

Who: Natalee, Steve, Kenneth, the Crandalls, Mrs. Devereaux.

What happens: Natalee learns that the car will cost too much to fix, and she should buy another. Kenneth left last night, angry with her, and she has probably lost him and the sales to the Crandalls by the Larkins. The show buying starts very slowly. She explains her financial situation to Steve, and he mentions a partnership. Mrs. Devereaux urges her to accept. The buying picks up. But near closing time Kenneth arrives and explains that the Crandalls called him to get in touch with Natalee. They want her to authenticate some of the items that the Larkins left with them. Kenneth tells her to authenticate them so that the Larkins will get the decorating job. Steve shows his disapproval. The Crandalls arrive and unwrap first a reproduction of a Tiffany vase, similar to the one Steve has.

Moment of revelation: She cannot go along with Kenneth. She places the fake by the genuine piece of Tiffany so even Kenneth can see the truth.

6. *Scene 5 (continued). Climax*

Purpose: To bring Natalee and Steve together.

When: At close of show.

Where: At the antiques show.

Who: Natalee, Steve, Kenneth, the Crandalls, Mrs. Devereaux.

What happens: Kenneth leaves in a huff. The Crandalls thank her and ask her to help them do their own decorating. Steve slips his arm around her, and she feels wonderful. Mrs. Devereaux smiles and nods approval. Natalee learns that sometimes you must listen to your heart instead of your head.

Take your plot summary and your character developments and expand them in the manner outlined above. Don't expect to do this blocking out in a matter of hours, but do continue until you finish. Make sure you have enough action in each scene to expand into the page limits suggested in Chapter 2.

Sometimes You Need a Scene Substitute

The beginner has a tendency to show everything in a scene no matter how unimportant the detail. The professional has learned that too many short scenes clutter your story and decrease the emotional impact. Reserve scenes for strong dramatic encounters and employ scene substitutes for minor events essential to the continuity of the action.

Scene substitutes get more mileage per word by summarizing the high points of unimportant events or by linking incidents in a *hindrance-furtherance arrangement*. In a hindrance incident the Viewpoint moves away from the solution to the problem, and a furtherance brings him closer to the solution.

Substitutes can actually replace some scenes, but not the crisis. Never substitute for the crisis.

1. The problem summary

If your critical situation lacks dramatic impact or color but the reader must know the facts to understand the story, summarize and move on to the more exciting first complication. This problem summary works well with a short-short—for example:

> Natalee Baxter had no way of knowing that a simple mix-up in assigning spaces at the antiques show would completely change the course of her life. Steve Atkins at the time meant no more to her than any other dealer at the show.

If you open this way, you want to summarize the climax, too:

> So Natalee told the truth about the vase, as Steve expected. Steve became the man in her life. She learned that sometimes you must listen to your heart instead of your head.

2. The first-person viewpoint summary

Instead of an opening scene, you let the Viewpoint, in characteristic narration, explain the problem situation to the reader:

> The way I look at it now, I might easily have sold the antiques business and become the wife of a partner in a real estate firm but for that silly mix-up on space assignments at the antiques show.
>
> Incidentally, I'm Natalee Baxter. My aunt who raised me died and left me her share of an antiques business. Aunt Harriet took me after my mother died and my father took off. We lived a sort of gypsy existence, as she called it, going from one show to the next and selling from our Victorian home only by appointment. I learned to identify antiques, and she handled the money. She insisted that I go to college and study art so I could make our exhibits more attractive.
>
> After college, I picked up where I left off, learning more and more about antiques so I could find sleepers and collectibles. Then Aunt Harriet died suddenly of a heart attack.

During those months after her death Kenneth Preston came to my aid quite by accident. He knocked on my door to see if I planned to sell the house. We dated regularly while I went through probate. He started talking marriage and real estate partnership at the same time. The only way we could manage a real estate partnership meant I should sell the business. He offered to help me find buyers for the antiques.

That's when the trouble started. Steve Atkins and I got assigned to the same spot at the show. As he pointed out, "We might as well help each other out of the jam and share the space." That's what we did. He even finished setting up while I went to meet the buyers.

As you can see, this type of opening won't do for our story, but I wanted to show you the device. If you open with Viewpoint summary, close the same way:

So I identified the vase as a fake in spite of what Kenneth wanted. But Steve cheered me on. That's when I realized that sometimes you must listen to your heart instead of your head. Steve and I got married. We still make the shows, but will slow down after the baby comes.

3. The hindrance-furtherance arrangement of incidents

If the Viewpoint trait dictates the plot action, you can open with a series of incidents in hindrance-furtherance arrangement and move on to the first complication. While you show no actual character conflict between two or more characters, the incidents give the flavor of a scene. You bind the incidents with a problem sentence and end with a decision. This example shows Natalee's indecision:

The day of the antiques show began the way her life had gone for the past few months after Aunt Harriet's death [binder sentence].

When she reached her assigned space to set up, a man

occupied it. "Looks like someone goofed," he said. "Guess we might as well share it. I'm Steve Atkins."

So they shared it. By the time she unpacked, Kenneth came by and said he could buy into a partnership at the real estate firm. "You can sell your antiques and let me have the money," he urged, and mentioned he had made an appointment for some buyers to come by her house that night. She agreed rather than argue.

But she didn't have time to finish setting up, so Steve suggested he could do it. She didn't want to trust him to do a good job, but she must so as to meet Kenneth [decision].

This type of scene substitute adapts especially well to a complication scene. You can easily cover a gap of time, touching only the high spots as in the second complication of our story. Since the device moves at a fast pace, you can substitute it for a scene immediately before the crisis. The action then slows for the more intensive drama of the crisis.

4. The dramatic-action substitute

Substitute this device for a complication scene when the Viewpoint interprets the action through inner conflict. Report only the action so that you bring the reader along with you to share it. Dramatic action differs from narration in that you project with action verbs, while narration tells. Open the action with a problem sentence, show the action, and end with a decision. Sometimes you may want to sandwich dramatic action in as an incident along with dialogue in a hindrance-furtherance arrangement.

In this example we take the reader on scene at the show with Natalee and Steve:

Natalee moved tensely to the foreground of the booth and crossed her fingers as the crowd funneled through the aisles of the show. This show could determine her entire future [binder sentence].

> A woman picked up the Tiffany vase. One look at the price, and she set it gently back in place. Steve grinned. Natalee turned her back on him.
>
> A man bought a stacked sugar and creamer signed "Heisey." Steve wrapped it and handed Natalee the money before he showed an old valentine to a customer. Lookers and buyers jammed the booth. They explained. They wrapped. They collected the money. At the lull, they both counted the money.
>
> If sales continued like this, she could afford the tune-up on the station wagon [decision].

This substitute scene moves very fast so it works well as a pacer. You may want to use it before the crisis to speed up the action.

5. *The implication ending*

A word saver adapted from television includes the implication ending. In a previous scene establish exactly what will happen if a certain event occurs. When the event happens, you need not spell out to the reader what will ensue. Do make the information as to the ending very graphic so the reader will not miss it and will recall it at the end. Otherwise, the reader may wonder what happened. This example shows how the device might work in our story:

> Natalee realized if she didn't work with the Larkins she might as well say farewell to Kenneth and any marriage plans. She could certainly make more in real estate than in selling antiques. But she knew antiques.

When Natalee doesn't back up the Larkins, Kenneth walks out. The reader supplies this ending for you have promised this would happen.

Expand your plot summary and characterization into scenes and scene substitutes where necessary. To write a scene in action, you must learn how to develop dialogue.

What Dialogue Can Do

If you think of dialogue as spoken words followed by an occasional "he said," you overlook about seventy percent of its emotional potential as a writing tool. *Bare* dialogue refers to the spoken words alone. *Full* dialogue includes the spoken words, all action relative to the spoken words, and the Viewpoint's thoughts and reactions.

Full Dialogue: When, Where, Who, What, and How

The full dialogue pattern consists of three distinct parts: who speaks, what he says, and how he says it. Remember these key words: *see*, *hear*, and *react*.

1. See the speaker

On television, the camera moves to focus on the next speaker. In the short story, you become the camera. Through action and reaction of the Viewpoint, or through action of the other characters, identify the speaker in the last sentence of the previous paragraph before he speaks. In the following paragraph, the identified person speaks. This arrangement makes each new paragraph begin with dialogue and gives a story the appearance of more spoken words than the story actually contains. Most readers prefer stories with short paragraphs and a large amount of dialogue. In this example, we begin with the last sentence of a paragraph:

> *Natalee looked at her watch and gasped.*
> "I must go or I'll not make it home in time for my appointment." She stopped right there. For some reason she didn't want to tell Steve about Kenneth and selling the business. *He carefully placed a valentine back of the Tiffany vase and stood back to admire it.*
> "It looks real pretty there; they sort of go together—the two things we don't want to sell," he said. *She ignored his last remark and reached for the last item in the box.*
> "I'll finish setting up in the morning," she said.

The italicized words identify the next speaker. Once we identify the two speakers, we can slip in a line without an identity. For variety, with a short pointer identify the speaker in the same paragraph with the spoken word:

> She closed the empty carton. "You can depend on me."
> He nodded. "I know I can."

Never let a character speak until you first show him to the reader. Sometimes a short paragraph of emotional reaction between spoken words intensifies the conflict as well as indicates the character who will speak next:

> Although she intended to keep the relationship strictly impersonal, she found this difficult. Steve seemed to guess what she wanted before she knew herself. This increased her worry about Kenneth's reaction to her sharing the space. He would never approve of Steve because he belonged to her world of antiques. Perhaps she shouldn't tell Kenneth. She started to lift a carton to the table, but Steve stopped her.
> "Let me do that. You do the arranging," he said.

When you first begin writing, you favor the more obvious ways to show the speaker, such as asking a question, addressing the next speaker, or omitting the identity and hoping a bare *"he said"* will do the job. Tags offer many possibilities, since they quickly project the individual speaker. These tags characterize as follows:

Action: Natalee chewed thoughtfully on her lip.

Speech: Kenneth almost choked on the words and turned an angry red.

Background: Steve placed his card with the address of his office near the cash register.

Sensory: Natalee softly, almost caressingly, ran her fingers over the Tiffany vase.

Mental: Natalee waited for Steve's usual logical comment.

Action always spotlights the speaker—as in "Steve gazed intently at the old valentine."

Introduce a different speaker with the spoken word:

"Here comes Mrs. Crandall now," Natalee nodded toward a woman carrying a large package.

"I want your advice," Mrs. Crandall said, and deposited the package on the chair by Natalee.

Identify the speaker by implication if the reader already knows the character. When dialogue reaches a high pitch of intensity at the crisis point of a scene, paragraphing implies the shift of speaker. The spoken words so characterize as to imply the identity: "Don't go lifting those heavy boxes" clearly points to Steve; "You know I love you," indicates Kenneth; "Honey, he's a real man" could come from no one but Mrs. Devereaux.

After three implications, resort to a strong point to the speaker.

In a story from a magazine you wish to sell, underline

with a red pencil all lines which point to the next speaker. Note the location of the pointer and identify the device.

2. Hear the speaker

In showing the speaker, you mainly identify the character for reader recognition. With the spoken word or bare dialogue, you intensify the character conflict. Bare dialogue in the present tense makes the reader feel the urgency of events happening right now. The spoken words emphasize the characterization in the point to the speaker by expressing the same emotion:

> Mrs. Crandall took the vase and smiled triumphantly.
> "I recognized it as a reproduction," she said, and her face reflected pride in her knowledge.

By overlapping the emotion, you intensify the conflict and hook the dialogue paragraphs together.

Not only do you restate the emotion but you order the words to fit the character. When the Viewpoint character thinks, his thoughts carry the same flavor as his spoken words.

Achieve naturalness in your spoken words by letting the characters speak with fragmentary sentences, broken-off thoughts finished with a gesture, dwindling words, or interrupting exclamations. Uninteresting chitchat or static bits add nothing to the story action. Each bit of bare dialogue should emphatically move the story forward.

When you write bare dialogue, go back and read the lines. Does each line develop the plot action? The spoken words give a vitamin pickup to your story. Select characterizing and stimulating words for the speaker, or twist worn phrases into new freshness and sparkle. Bare dialogue should punch dramatically, extract a tear or a chuckle, and thoroughly entertain your reader.

3. Project the reaction

In the third step of full dialogue, trace the rising conflict between the characters with "*he said.*" The word *said* conveys an emotionless fact. As the conflict becomes more heated, insert an adverb or an adjectival phrase to show emotionally *how* the character said the words, as "*he said hotly.*" A *said* substitute, like "*he shouted,*" implies even stronger emotion. At the crisis peak of the scene, drop the *said* entirely for the strongest emotion. In this manner, the *said* and the spoken words move the characters through an emotional revolution:

he said:	"he said"
he said how:	"he said hotly"
he said substitute:	"he shouted"
no he said:	"I dare you"
he said:	"he said"

The *said* revolution may begin at any point and move in any direction with any combination. At times you may need only a part of the revolution. This revolution would project a character who moves from cold to hot:

he said
he said how
he said
he said substitute

Move from a slow *said* gradually to the *no said* to show a character with good control of himself. Your material and the point in the story sequence and the scene, as well as your character himself, determine the *said* revolution.

The *said* carries the same emotion as the identity pointer and the spoken word. Thus you project the same emotion three times. This identical emotion may continue for several paragraphs, or it can shift in the dialogue paragraph with the Viewpoint's reaction and the point to the next speaker. Too many *said substitutes* or *no he saids* weaken dramatic effectiveness. Build to them with the *said* and *said how*.

So in writing full dialogue, identify the speaker, let him speak in the next paragraph, tell how he speaks, then point to the next speaker. Continue the process until you create a *scene cycle* that projects the emotional conflict you desire.

How Dialogue Moves a Scene

Every story has two forward movements: a cycle within the scene and a sequence of events in the plot pattern. Dialogue creates the forward movement in the scene cycle, presenting characters in conflict:

1. The choice of characters

Choose all characters deliberately to agree or disagree with the Viewpoint. If you draw characters who disagree, they automatically start the scene cycle with a conflict of opinion:

Mrs. Larkin stepped back and examined the oak cabinet from various directions.

"Lovely, lovely," she said, "but it certainly needs refinishing."

Natalee disagreed. "You'll destroy the old patina," she said bluntly. Her dislike for Mrs. Larkin spiraled.

2. The type of conflict

To add emotional momentum to the forward cycle of the scene, fit the *said* revolution to the three types of conflict: mental, physical, and emotional. When a character resorts to mental conflict—argues, reasons, or gives information—*said* works best. With emotional conflict, such as persuasion, add *how* to the *said*. If the character threatens or tries physical force, a *said substitute* or *no he said* projects the emotion best:

Steve looked at the price on the blue collector's plate. "Looks like you price hit or miss," he said.

"Not necessarily," she said coolly, and marked a price on a pressed glass pitcher.

"You can tell a lot about a dealer by the way he prices. If he goes too high, he wants to keep it," he said confidently. "If he puts it too cheaply, everybody thinks something's wrong with it."

"So I suppose you put a fair price on everything," Natalee snapped.

"I try."

"But you can't."

"Why not?"

"You may put a cheap price on it because you bought it for less, or you have kept it in stock a long time," she said, wanting to end the conversation. For two cents she would pack up her things and leave him with a half-empty space right now.

Note that the scene begins with "*said*," since one character, Steve, gives information that upsets the other character, Natalee. The conflict picks up with "*said coolly*." Then Natalee "*snapped*," and we reach the bare dialogue. Natalee winds up the conversation. The inner thoughts and reactions slow the momentum.

3. *The type of dialogue*

To the character conflict and the *said* development, add the shift from full to bare dialogue. With the *said*, let the reader see, hear, and react to the characters. As the conflict grows with the *said how*, reduce the amount of Viewpoint thinking and reaction. The *said substitute* drops everything but the *said*. Bare dialogue omits even the *said*.

Bare dialogue occurs only at intensely dramatic points of strong conflict, using only two to three lines at a time to preserve its dramatic effectiveness. Reverse this process to move back to the *said* or full dialogue.

4. The Paragraphing

Paragraphing offers a mechanical forward movement. Each time a different person speaks, make a new paragraph. This gives the reader a feeling of progression and avoids confusion with regard to the speaker. But Viewpoint reaction which indicates the Viewpoint as the next speaker comes in the paragraph with the other character's spoken words. If you use a long reaction, place it in a separate paragraph.

In each paragraph of your story, move from emotion to motion, or from reaction to action.

> Natalee fought the urge to tell Mrs. Crandall how she truly felt about the Larkins. She didn't want to sell a single item to the decorators no matter how much Kenneth needed the money. She took Mrs. Crandall to the bedroom on pretense of showing her an antique.

The first sentence shows Natalee's dislike of the Larkins and her protective feeling for Mrs. Crandall. The last sentence projects action to do something about the situation.

You may suggest action negatively, as, "She must not act anxious," or imply future probability, as, "If she acted the least bit anxious, they would assume she needed to sell." The shift to a new emotion comes right before the action, but the same emotion often continues for several paragraphs:

> Natalee wanted to upset the Larkins' plans, but smoothly. She tried to get Kenneth into the kitchen, but Mrs. Larkin took his arm and led him away.
> She determined more than ever to find a way to ruin

their plans. Perhaps Steve could give her an idea. She began to ease him toward the front door, but Mrs. Larkin stopped them to ask him a question.

Natalee didn't intend to let Mrs. Larkin outsmart her. She spotted Mrs. Crandall near the bedroom door, so she pretended to get Kenneth's attention. Again Mrs. Larkin stepped between them. Triumphantly, Natalee took Mrs. Crandall's arm and led her into the bedroom.

The emotion stays the same—break up the plans—until the third paragraph when Natalee wins. Note the action at the end of each paragraph gives conflict and forward movement.

5. The scene sequence

How much forward movement a scene cycle needs depends on its location in the action sequence. The opening scene usually has a fast pace to catch the reader's interest. This means a complete scene cycle. Arrange the complication scenes to slow, then speed up, then slow, and again speed up the action. Slow the action with full dialogue, and speed it up with bare dialogue.

The crisis scene begins slowly but gathers momentum as it moves to the moment of revelation, where it slows again. The climax moves very fast.

The types of conflict used in a scene may affect the pace as well as the rate at which the Viewpoint makes a decision. The right combination of these pacing devices within the scene and within the action sequence instigates the up and down emotion of fiction.

In summary, these five devices work together to produce the scene cycle. Study stories in several magazines and underline examples of devices which create forward movement in the story along with the decisions of the major character. Basically, a story travels on the decisions of the Viewpoint.

Spicing Dialogue with Variety

Beginning writers tend to let their characters make long speeches when first writing dialogue. This encourages the reader to skim or skip. Or else they write the speeches all the same length and create monotonous reading. Variety adds spice to dialogue, and the following devices stimulate interest:

1. Short interruptions

Make one character talkative and the other timid. The talkative one begins a windy oration, and the timid one interrupts with 'But I—" or "Oh, no!" The talker waves aside the interruptions and continues. This not only breaks up a long speech containing facts the reader must know, but it also increases the conflict. Eventually, the interrupting character will explode and say his bit while the talker remains quiet.

2. Thought transfer

Too often in writing dialogue, beginning writers shy away from including the Viewpoint's thoughts and reactions, putting everything into the spoken word, in this manner:

> "I'm perfectly capable of selling antiques, and I don't need any suggestions from you," she said bluntly. "I've probably been selling longer and forgotten more than you ever knew. I'm only sharing the space and not my business."

Let's transfer part of this to her thoughts:

> "I'm perfectly capable of selling antiques, and I don't need any suggestions from you," she said bluntly. She'd

probably forgotten more than he ever knew. "I'm only sharing the space and not the business."

The second example has more suspense because the reader wonders if Natalee might change her mind about Steve, since she doesn't say all she thinks. The fewer spoken words give some action but greatly increase reader identification by confiding the Viewpoint's thoughts. It adds emotional suspense by withholding her true thoughts from Steve.

3. Emotional action

A character does not need to speak. His actions say more than any words and dramatize the emotional conflict:

> "I can't buy a van. I'm almost broke," she confessed.
> Steve shrugged.
> "I haven't sold anything for months. I've been tied up in probate," she added.
> He looked into the milling crowd.
> "I may sell out or go into bankruptcy." As a lawyer, he would understand that.

Without speaking a word, Steve makes Natalee reconsider selling the antiques business.

4. Narration

In giving background information or referring to a previous event, start with dialogue and shift to rapid narration. Return to dialogue at the end.

> "I may have a buyer for some of my antiques," Natalee began calmly, but the next minute she poured out the entire story of how Kenneth planned to use the Larkins and the Crandalls to get money for the real estate partnership. "I feel so guilty, doing this to that nice Mrs. Crandall."

The narration reminds the reader of the Viewpoint's

motive for selling the business. This device lifts the narration to the same emotional impact as the spoken words but does not burden the reader by repeating details already given.

5. *Conflict revolution*

For greater conflict, start the Viewpoint and the other character at a different emotional step in the said revolution. While one remains calm, the other grows angry:

> "I don't like the Larkins," she sobbed. Kenneth took a step closer to her.
> "Get hold of yourself. You haven't recovered from your aunt's death," he said. "It takes time."
> "You blame everything on Aunt Harriet," she stormed.
> "You're upset," he said, and put his arm around her.
> She flung it off. "You keep talking me into things you want to do," she accused.
> "I'm only thinking of your best interest," he said softly. "I want to look after you."

Write some dialogue for your characters and apply these suggestions.

What Dialogue Must Do

In a stage play an actor or actress can breathe life into poor dialogue with a tone of voice, facial expression, or characteristic actions or gestures. The writer cannot expect this help. You must put into your dialogue all that the actor or actress could do for the playwright. Your dialogue must stand on its own to your audience, the reader. To accomplish this, each line of dialogue must perform several functions:

1. *To characterize*

Dialogue characterization succeeds only if you

project a clear picture of the Viewpoint and the supporting characters by what they say. The Viewpoint thinks and speaks as his trait, tag, and motivation so direct. A supporting character speaks and acts as you have programmed. Strive for each character to speak as an individual and get rid of any sameness.

You can achieve good character projection by contrast or comparison shown in spoken words. We contrast Natalee's indecision with Steve's logic:

> Steve looked thoughtful. "Supposing the Crandalls don't fall for the scheme?" Natalee shook her head.
> "But they did," she insisted. Her guilt grew more depressing by the minute. "A dealer should have integrity."
> "What if they force me?" she asked.
> "Then don't sell to the Larkins," he advised.
> "I'll defend you. Why not talk with the Crandalls?" he reasoned.
> "And let them know I tried to cheat them?" The situation grew worse by the minute.

A reversal also gives good characterization. Let one character begin and the other finish the speech:

> Kenneth looked disturbed over Natalee's reaction to the Larkins. "They're knowledgeable, artistic and—"
> "Sharpies," Natalee added.

Let the character speak through the lingo of his job but in terms any reader can understand. Kenneth would say, "I only want to help you liquidate your assets and give you more tangible security." These words characterize the sophisticated abstract terminology of banking or real estate. The reader comes to expect Kenneth to talk this way as the story develops.

2.   *To give background information*

Weave the background information through the full dialogue so that these necessary facts do not stop your story action. Story action always takes priority over narration. Beginners write this way:

> "So you like to work with antiques," Steve said.
> Natalee had worked with antiques as far back as she could remember. Her aunt took her to shows as a child. She sat her in a little chair in the booth. She talked with people and learned about antiques. She knew no other way of life.
> "I certainly do," she agreed.

The professional projects the information something like this:

> "So you like to work with antiques," Steve said.
> "I don't know any other life," she said. She thought of the little rocking chair Aunt Harriet put in the booth for her. From that moment on she became a part of the business, listening to adults talk about antiques and learning all the time.

Always color facts with Viewpoint reaction:

> "I like doing shows." She found a challenge in packing a fragile figurine to preserve its perfection and displaying it so people stopped and stared. She knew the joy of returning from a show with nothing broken. "It's my heritage."

Specifics and strong emotion make the reader care about the Viewpoint. If you sandwich background narration between bare dialogue, hit the high emotional points which will strengthen the motivation and point to future action. Never load the spoken words with facts the other character already knows:

"Kenneth, you are a successful real estate salesman who works with people who need houses, the necessities of life. You can't understand about antiques."

Study this emotional face-lift:

As a successful real estate salesman, Kenneth thought only of the essentials of life: food, clothing, and especially shelter. He could easily compute, understand these needs. "You've never set your heart on owning one small thing of beauty, one special figurine," she tried to make him understand, "and willingly made sacrifices."

The Viewpoint's reaction to the dialogue and motives of the supporting characters can emphasize background:

"Give the Larkins a chance," Kenneth urged. "Think of our marriage plans."

"Our plans," she repeated with emphasis. From the first date he talked of nothing but selling her "junk" as if it imprisoned her, of getting away from the tawdry life of the antiques show circuit. "I'm thinking very hard," she said. She must find a way out of this mess with the Larkins.

3. To intensify the conflict

Dialogue emphasizes the Viewpoint's struggle to solve the problem. This struggle consists of an inner and outer conflict. Interweave the two conflicts through the dialogue of the scene. The Viewpoint may speak one way and think another:

"I hope we never have to put up with each other again," Natalee declared, but she didn't mean it. She already depended on him too much.

Force the character to talk under stress:

"You must tell the Crandalls," Steve insisted, looking deep into her eyes.

"What would the Larkins do to Kenneth?" she asked and thought of all sorts of terrible things. They might even get him fired.

"Are you in love with him?"

She bit her lower lip, searching frantically for an answer. "I think so."

Steve reached for her hand. "And you plan to marry him?"

"I don't know. I don't know," she said too quickly. "It's none of your business."

Develop conflict in identifying the speaker, in the *said* revolution, in character action, and in Viewpoint reaction.

4. *To advance the plot action*

As previously discussed in this chapter, dialogue—both in the scene cycle and in the action sequence—advances the story toward a solution. Each bit of dialogue adds conflict and pushes the Viewpoint to make new decisions to solve the problem.

To identify ineffective dialogue in your writing, go through a scene reading only the spoken words of one character at a time. Static dialogue will stand out—for elimination.

5. *To create suspense*

Dialogue creates suspense by pointing to coming events and by picking up previous plants. Finally, Natalee's old car refused to start, a previous plant, and Steve joins her:

"Don't worry another minute," Steve said, helping Natalee into his van. "I'll call this friend of mine. He'll come get your car, have it purring like a kitten."

"But does he work on Sunday?" she said, wondering how to get back to the show.

"I represented him in a little trouble. He'll fix it for me," Steve assured. "And I'll transport you tomorrow."

The reader wonders if the car will get fixed. Would this new problem push her to sell the business?

Dialogue suspensefully reveals the Viewpoint's choice of action as well as his innermost feelings. Suspense emphasizes the *when* and *how* a situation will work rather than withholding detail about the *what*. If you withhold from your reader a fact your Viewpoint knows to achieve a surprise, you'll get criticism—not acclaim.

Suspense results from letting the reader wonder if the Viewpoint can continue hiding facts from another character or denying what she actually feels:

> At a lull in the show, Steve went to visit with other dealers. Natalee collapsed in the nearest chair. Mrs. Devereaux joined her.
>
> "He's in love with you," she said.
>
> "That's ridiculous! No one falls in love overnight or in two days," she denied, and yet Steve stayed uppermost in her mind.
>
> "You like him, too," she stated, cocking her head to one side. Natalee met her insinuation with a steady gaze.
>
> "I hardly know him," she said. Mrs. Devereaux picked up a bisque figurine of young lovers and studied it. "Ah, love, how very blind you are!"

6. *To wind up loose ends*

The wordage of the short story does not permit you to give every little detail of the action. So you rely on dialogue to keep the reader and the Viewpoint up-to-date on what happens to other characters in the story. In like manner the Viewpoint may bring other characters up-to-date on her activities:

> Steve fumbled with the old valentine. "About your car. I got up early this morning and went over and talked to my friend," he said, and kept smoothing the lacy paper that framed the heart.

"When will he get it fixed?" She unwrapped a cut glass bowl and made room for it on a side table.

Steve slowly replaced the valentine behind the Tiffany vase. "He says it's not worth fixing. But he has a bargain in a secondhand van. It won't cost much more than having your old car fixed, and you'll have good transportation."

7. To create a mood

While most stories have a dominant emotional tone, it varies between high and low moods. When the major character sinks into a depression or feels elated, the dialogue can project these moods. The other characters also experience mood changes:

Mrs. Devereaux moved the little Hummel boy closer to the girl figurine. "Steve reminds me so much of my first husband," she sighed deeply.

Natalee tried not to sound annoyed. "In what way?"

"Mr. Merriweather used to help me at the shows the way Steve does for you." She rambled on for several seconds. "There never was a more lovable man." She seemed lost in her memories. "Some people never appreciate a person until he's gone—I mean fully appreciate."

Natalee thought of Aunt Harriet, the shows they worked together. "I know what you mean," she said softly.

"Then why don't you do something about that dear boy?" She grinned shyly.

Successful writing means correct practice, so test your own skill in writing functional dialogue for your story. While each example basically serves one specific purpose, you cannot eliminate other functions completely. Read your dialogue line by line and make sure it accomplishes at least two functions. Prove to yourself the fun and profit in writing dialogue with a purpose, then you can concentrate on writing the first pages of your story.

Those Challenging First Pages

We have reached the most exciting stage in creating a short story—writing the problem situation. You can't dash it off! No one does, for the problem situation forms the foundation upon which you build the rest of the story. It begins with an opening hook and ends with the Viewpoint's first decision to solve the problem.

Within this scope you, the storyteller, must build an illusion of reality that starts the adventure for the Viewpoint. Here lies the real challenge. Like a jigsaw puzzle you must carefully fit together these nine essentials all stories use in the right places to form the complete picture:

Hook, Bait, and Grabber

The first few paragraphs of a short story contain the *hook*, *bait*, or *grabber*. These paragraphs catch the reader's attention and stimulate him to read the story. To achieve this purpose, the hook predicts the type of story, sets the dominant emotional tone, and establishes the line of continuity. The type of hook determines the amount of information you need to convey and the market slant.

1. The summary hook

The summary hook introduces the Viewpoint, hints at the problem or character trait, pegs the setting, promises conflict, and suggests the emotional tone. Often this type of hook suggests the immediacy and identifies the gimmick. To do all these things may seem an impossibility, but concentrated work and well-chosen words can accomplish it.

With so much included in this hook, it shortens the problem situation and allows the story to move rapidly to the first complication. In a short-short, the summary hook actually replaces the critical situation, and the story skips on to the first complication. But make sure that the Viewpoint and not the author does the summary.

This illustration shows how an author's summary diminishes the emotion and loses reader identification:

> The death of an aunt completely disrupted Natalee Baxter's life. At the antiques show she ran into another disturbing situation with Steve Atkins that would erase many of her plans with Kenneth Preston.

To get rid of the author in the driver's seat of a summary hook, let the Viewpoint introduce himself, state the problem, and predict the conflict. While this type of hook runs longer and slows the pace, it either completely eliminates the problem situation or cuts it in half:

> When Natalee Baxter arrived to set up at the antiques show, she thought she had narrowed all the problems caused by Aunt Harriet's death to a single one. Certainly she would know by the end of the show whether or not she would sell the business. But nothing prepared her for the meeting with Steve Atkins.

Some editors feel that readers prefer third-person viewpoint because the first person often sounds brash and conceited. If you find an editor who does want the more conservative third-person viewpoint, then substitute *she* for *I*.

The first-person viewpoint summary hook works best with a light or humorous story if you open with the problem or in a high dramatic story which stresses the Viewpoint's strong trait. In the opening sentence establish the trait, use the present tense to give the flavor of "I am this way" and the sharing quality so necessary with first person. After you establish the trait, the story continues in the active past:

> I am the kind of person who hates to make decisions, so I left them to Aunt Harriet. Her death threw me into a panic, but by setup time at the antiques show, I faced only one problem: whether or not to sell the business. In fact, I more or less made up my mind to sell. Then I met Steve Atkins.

With the third person you use the active past entirely, along with your change in pronoun. The summary hook, then, works with either situation or character story.

Men like the summary hook because they want to get immediately into the action. Women prefer a slower, more emotional buildup than men. For either reader the hook always reveals the Viewpoint's problem.

2. The action hook

This type of hook shows the Viewpoint in action which explains and successfully develops into the main conflict of the story:

> Natalee Baxter drove the old station wagon into the building and prepared to unpack the antiques. But a strange man already occupied the space. "You have the wrong space," she said, handing him her ticket.

He reached into the pocket of his plaid shirt and took out a similar tag. "Nope, this is the right one," he said, and handed her the slips.

"Someone gave us the same space," she said, ready to burst into tears. She spent all day yesterday building up her confidence to do the show without Aunt Harriet, and then this happened.

"I'm sure we can work this out. I'm Steve Atkins," he extended his hand.

Action always keeps the reader reading. This hook favors the situation story.

3. The character trait

In the first sentence of the hook, introduce the right and wrong facet of the Viewpoint's trait by thoughts or action. Let the trait create the conflict:

Natalee Baxter's life became one urgent decision after the other following her aunt's death. What she judged as right, turned her life into chaos. What she thought as wrong, worked. At the moment she had reached the point of total confusion about everything.

As discussed in Chapter 6, under scene substitutes, a variation of the character hook shows the trait in a series of hindrance-furtherance incidents before the story action begins. When you emphasize the Viewpoint's trait in the hook, you indicate a character story or a combination of situation-character.

4. The setting hook

Any time environment influences the Viewpoint's action, link the setting with the conflict in the story:

For a moment Natalee Baxter stood in the empty building and soaked up the familiar sounds of setting up an antiques show. Exhaust fumes mingled with the aroma of perking coffee. Shouts and laughter rose above the hammering or banging of folded tables. In a matter of hours the chaos would metamorphize into glittering exhibits. Yet she wondered how long she could continue as a part of this scene she knew so well and loved.

5. The theme hook

This hook shows the negative and the positive facet of the theme as it applies to the Viewpoint's problem or trait. Give enough facts to catch the reader, but not so many that you destroy the suspense of the story:

> Natalee Baxter maintained that financial security should come first in considering marriage, but Steve insisted two people must love each other. Together they created the security. Kenneth would certainly never agree.

At the conclusion of the story Natalee learns that sometimes you must listen to your heart. The theme hook works well with any type of story but best with those that emphasize character trait.

6. The frame hook

For the frame hook, you select an interesting or exciting place in the forward action and open at that point; then you present the story chronologically as it happened. Three specialized situations indicate this type of hook. In a minor character viewpoint story where the major one dies, use a frame. Unless you notify the reader of the death, he will feel disappointed at the conclusion.

Television developed another type of hook to hold the viewer through the first commercial. The screen shows a very short dramatic bit from the opening of the crisis, then comes the commercial. After the commercial, the story starts with the problem situation and moves to the climax, skipping the part of the crisis previously shown.

The short story writer takes a few paragraphs from the beginning of the crisis to hook the reader, then goes back and tells the story chronologically. Naturally, you skip over the part of the crisis you have already used. This frame hook usually opens a situation story.

In another type of frame hook the Viewpoint meets a person from the past and then remembers the circumstances of the last encounter. You'll find this type more often in women's magazines or with the nostalgic article.

Regardless of your purpose, beware of the pitfalls. Do not give so much information that you anticlimax the suspense of the story. By all means keep the hook fast paced, but let it glide into the beginning of the story so the reader feels no interruption:

> Natalee Baxter held the small vase tightly in her hand and pretended to examine it. She tried to ignore Steve who stood there like a prosecuting attorney.
> Kenneth made no effort to hide his impatience. "Go ahead, tell her who made it!" he urged.
> Her whole future depended on her authentication of this Tiffany vase. The problem really started three days ago with a mix-up in spaces at the antiques show.

We pull this hook from the middle of the crisis scene and then transition to the opening of the story to tell it chronologically.

These depict the pure forms of the basic hooks. Your creativeness comes with combining or blending these hooks for originality and emotional impact. Combine trait with setting or theme for a character story. Use action and Viewpoint summary for a situation story.

In the Natalee story we will combine setting and trait

in a series of incidents leading up to the mix-up in spaces. Such a combination makes a longer hook:

> Natalee Baxter double-parked the old station wagon in front of the check-in office at the fairgrounds. Halfway out of the car she remembered that Aunt Harriet strongly disapproved of dealers who double-parked. She slid back under the wheel and took a nearby space.
>
> Inside the building, Natalee joined the moving line to the desk with her space notice in hand. Having the same space and same antiques dealers on either side would help a lot. The loudspeaker system suddenly blasted the air: "Space 50 needs 4 tables. Space 50 needs 4 tables." She mentally pictured the number of tables she needed, 4 or 5? The woman reached for Natalee's notice.
>
> "Yesterday morning they shifted the show to a different building." She fumbled through the file box three times before she pulled out a card. "I sat up most of the night making new assignments."
>
> A different space, new dealers—how could she possibly manage alone?
>
> "I'm short of spaces. If you want to cancel—"
>
> "I guess I'll take it." She took the floor plan and directions to the exhibition building.

These incidents not only show Natalee's trait of indecision, but they also give the setting and point to the mix-up in space assignments. Your material will suggest the most successful combination for your story.

The Other Eight Essentials

As soon as you have written the hook for your story, go to work on the other eight essentials that form the foundation of your story. If you thoroughly develop these essentials in the problem situation, the remainder of the story will almost write itself:

1. Setting

All stories rely on a basic setting with contingent

places where other scenes occur. All through the action and the thoughts of the Viewpoint, work in details of the basic setting and nearby places in the problem situation. In this way the setting becomes so vivid in the reader's mind that a few well-chosen words can establish the contingent setting in each new scene.

Setting does more than describe the place where the action occurs. It can help the hook establish the dominant emotional tone, suggest the type of characters who will appear, create the social atmosphere, indicate the time of day. When you write setting, interweave bits and pieces into the action of the characters and reactions of the Viewpoint so you don't stop the forward movement of the story:

> Steve set *the carton of antiques on the cement floor.* Natalee pulled out a *Haviland platter.* Mrs. Devereaux *leaned over the partition.* "You sold a lot yesterday, didn't you?"
> Natalee nodded and handed the *platter* to Steve. *He placed it upright behind the set of doll dishes.*
> Mrs. Devereaux *came around to the entrance of the booth.* "That really looks nice."
> Another dealer *leaned over the counter on the right.* "How much for *the churn in the corner?*"

The italicized words mark the setting pegs worked into the action. The Natalee story takes place at an antiques show in San Francisco and in a Victorian house in the same area. The show adds to the emotional tone of romance. All the characters relate to the show in some way.

2. Characters

In the problem situation introduce all the characters who appear in the story. Bring in nonappearing characters by name or profession.

Sometimes you can imply a nonappearing character by a relationship, such as a customer; a place, like an antiques show; or a coming event, such as an appointment to sell antiques.

The Viewpoint always appears first to establish the basic problem growing out of the situation or the trait. Present all supporting characters one at a time in relation to the right or wrong course for the Viewpoint in the solution of the problem. The positive supporting character should come on scene before the negative one, implying their function and attitude toward the Viewpoint's problem. The theme character may or may not appear in the opening scene, but the background character should come in early. Introduce other minor characters as needed to intensify the conflict.

By the end of the problem situation, the reader must know the trait, tag, function, ability, and motivation of the Viewpoint and the two supporting characters. Project them so clearly that a key word will present the total picture later in the story. Once the action begins, you must not stop for new characterization.

In the Natalee story, we introduce the Viewpoint first, then Steve and finally Kenneth. Kenneth mentions the Larkins. The implication that the Larkins have customers suggests the Crandalls. Mrs. Devereaux appears in the opening scene.

Natalee's problem consists of whether or not to sell the antiques business. This involves her in a love triangle with Steve, who represents the positive, and Kenneth, who represents the negative.

3. Immediacy

Immediacy creates urgency for action and heightens the suspense of the story. As soon as possible, establish how long the Viewpoint has to work out a solution to the problem. A short duration produces more suspense than a longer one, but keep it plausible. Mention the immediacy in the hook and develop its importance in the problem situation. At the decision point, this immediacy pushes the Viewpoint into action to solve the problem.

The problem situation establishes the total time for the story action. Each scene must happen within this time limit.

Our story opens on Friday afternoon and ends on Sunday near closing time of the show.

4. Conflict

Conflict grows out of the Viewpoint's problem, which results from the situation or the trait. Make the problem so vital to the Viewpoint's welfare that he must act at once or find himself engulfed by disaster. From this problem evolve the three basic conflicts of the story: inner, outer, and environmental.

The right and wrong of the Viewpoint's trait determines the amount of inner and outer conflict. He wants inwardly to do what he believes right but finds the wrong path more tempting. This inner turmoil expresses itself through the Viewpoint's conflict with other characters who urge him to take the right or wrong turn.

Any new conflict situation brought into the story must grow out of the main or supporting conflicts introduced in the problem situation. So check your conflicts and see if you introduced them all in the problem situation.

Natalee must decide whether or not to sell the antiques business and invest in the real estate firm for Kenneth. Steve involves her in a triangle that combines love and career. Natalee wants to continue the business as Steve advises, but with Kenneth's urging, she keeps deciding to sell. So the problem situation introduces the career and love with a promise of other personal conflicts with the Larkins.

5. Suspense

Suspense grows out of the Viewpoint's decisions to solve the problem. Consequently the problem must offer numerous right and wrong decisions, as well as several ways to expand the Viewpoint's emotional horizons at the moment of revelation. To create suspense properly, you must know how much the Viewpoint will change and what solution will bring the Viewpoint and the positive supporting character together. This knowledge enables you to hint at the possible solution and pull the Viewpoint in the conflicting directions of the problem situation.

While the reader feels confident the Viewpoint will solve the problem in the time allowed, he does not guess how. The plausibility of the solution depends on the clarity of your plants and pointers in the problem situation. Never let anything merely happen—build to it. Plant the gimmick-symbol, facts, people, motives, and conditions which create suspense. Point to what might or might not happen in future scenes. Once you build the reader's expectations, fulfill them, but not in the way that the reader expected. Suspense comes not from shocking your reader with new information, but from keeping him overinformed, so he makes the wrong guess.

We know that Natalee will discover Steve as the right man for her and will not sell the business. We suggest the difference between the reproduction and the genuine Tiffany early in the story when Steve has a fake.

We point out that Natalee and Steve know and like dealing in antiques. Natalee likes Steve but feels indebted to Kenneth who has helped her so much. When Natalee leaves the setting-up to Steve, you expect something to go wrong. Her indecision about the Larkins points to possible conflict there, involving the Crandalls.

6. Motivation

Through solid or scattered flashback, establish clearly the basic motivation for the Viewpoint and all the supporting characters.

Natalee hopes to continue with the business, but she also wants to help Kenneth. Steve likes Natalee and wants to become the man in her life. We need only scattered flashback. The chapter on motivation covered this part thoroughly.

7. Decision

The problem situation ends when the Viewpoint goes over his choices for action and makes a decision which he hopes will solve the problem immediately. The basic decision sets off a chain reaction of choices which do not end until the moment of revelation. So all future decisions stem from this basic one. Remember, the story moves forward on the decisions.

Steve agrees to finish setting up the booth. Natalee goes to meet the Larkins, putting her in the negative.

8. Dominant emotion

If you proportion the eight preceding elements correctly, you will achieve the dominant emotion. Romance creates the dominant emotion of love in the Natalee story.

Keep in mind these nine essentials when you write

the first draft of the problem situation. Put the manuscript aside for at least a week while you think of possible revisions. Make any necessary changes at the end of the week.

Using your scene summary, write the remainder of your story, but not at one sitting. Carefully think through a scene and write it. Then wait until the next day before you write the next scene. Always make a copy of the first draft of your story and file away for future use. As you did for the problem situation, let this first draft cool.

When you take your story out of objective storage, you can make it read like one big adventure with smooth transitioning.

Continuity Spells Sales

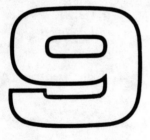

A short story with good continuity usually sells quickly.

Although you unfold a story in units of paragraphs and scenes with necessary changes in time, place, and emotion, all must knit together so tightly the reader finds no break until the end. If you transition these natural breaks with the appropriate devices, your story will read as one big adventure.

Transitions: The Vital Link

Most short stories make three basic changes between scenes: *time, place,* and *emotion.* Now and then you will transition viewpoint, but this technique applies more to the novel or novelette. To transition these necessary changes, link the old with the new.

1. *Time and place*

The problem situation of your story establishes an immediacy or time duration within which the Viewpoint must solve the problem. Each scene moves the Viewpoint nearer to this deadline of the crisis. A simple arrangement of words links the old time and place with the new ones.

In the last paragraph of the scene, preferably in one last sentence, indicate the present place and time period, and, if possible, imply the new ones. The first sentence of the next paragraph in the new scene establishes the time lapse and change of place:

> Natalee halfway hoped the Crandalls wouldn't like her antiques, but that must wait until tomorrow, she reminded herself, and tried to get some sleep.
>
> The next morning worry about the Crandalls completely left her mind when she saw the way Steve had set up the exhibit at the show.

The time lapse extends from bedtime one night to the following morning. The place moves from the home to the show.

2. Time

Each new scene requires a transition in time but not always a change in place. Make the transition in time exactly as you did the one in time and place:

> Around five in the afternoon at the show, the crowd began to dwindle. Natalee checked on how much she would need to bring to the show the next day to restock. Steve went to check on starting the car.
>
> He returned thirty minutes later and shook his head. "The battery's dead."

Only the time changes in this incident, as all the action stays at the show in the exhibit. With a shift in time you can often hurdle a day or two and move on to the next exciting action. You maintain the time continuity of the story but highlight the dramatic spots.

3. Emotion

While you transition time and place at the end of one

scene and the beginning of the next, emotion changes only in the middle of a paragraph and may shift several times during the scene. If you change the emotion at the beginning of the new scene, in addition to time, place, and paragraph break, you encourage the reader to lay the story aside.

Think of the temptations facing the reader as he turns the pages of the magazine: the enticing advertisements, the other feature stories, and eye-catching illustrations. He may quit reading your story if you don't grip him emotionally. Strong emotional continuity combats these temptations. Consequently, the last sentence of one paragraph always carries the same or a similar emotion as that of the first line in the new paragraph:

> Selling the antiques business would greatly help Kenneth, and she should want to help her future husband.
>
> Once he owned the partnership, they could get married with this financial security. She wouldn't need to worry about finding antiques, going to shows—she stopped right there. She wondered if she could so abruptly change her life, turn her back on antiques after all of Aunt Harriet's efforts and training.

The first paragraph ends with the decision to sell. This decisiveness continues until the middle of the next paragraph when indecisiveness takes over. This emotion may continue for another paragraph before you shift to the new emotion in the middle of the paragraph.

The emotional transition in dialogue comes immediately after the *said*:

> "Help the Larkins," she said almost to herself. No way. "They don't need help, but their victims do."
>
> "If you don't help, you could spoil my future," Kenneth reminded.

Natalee appears stunned, then rebels. Kenneth continues the rebellious mood. In full dialogue where you give whole paragraphs of Viewpoint reaction between spoken words, transition in the middle of the mood paragraph:

> Spoil his future? What about her life? She thought of Aunt Harriet and how hard she worked to build up this business. She thought of giving up everything for Kenneth. He never considered what she wanted—only his own ambition. She should think of herself and what she wanted.
>
> "I'm not selling," she said confidently.

In this example, the spoken words have more impact because of the emotional buildup in the intervening paragraph. The emotion starts with stunned silence and shifts to a positive refusal.

Checking each emotional transition takes time and concentration, but it will guarantee the unified action editors buy.

4. Viewpoint

If you have chosen a dual viewpoint for your short story, you must transition from one character to the next only between the scenes. In the last sentence of the paragraph, bring the new Viewpoint on scene with the present one. In the first sentence of the next paragraph, along with the change in time, place, and scene, shift to the new viewpoint:

> Natalee and Steve totaled the sales for the day. They far exceeded her expectations. At this rate she might manage to pay for a much needed tune-up on the car.
>
> Steve wondered how he could break the news gently to Natalee that the car needed far more than a tune-up.

In the first paragraph Natalee performs as the viewpoint. In the second, Steve takes over. Unless your material demands dual viewpoint, don't shift back and forth between the characters.

Shifting viewpoint requires too many words for clarity and loses self-identification and continuity, thereby confusing the editor and the reader.

Check your story for transitions in time, place, and emotion. When you know how to make these three changes, you take only the first step in transitioning a story. The scenes need linking with a *red string of continuity* that weaves in and out of the story action:

Red Strings Tie Your Story Together

While good transitioning in time, place, and emotion helps to dovetail scenes, you need assistance from other devices as well—devices which string the scenes together like a strand of beads.

Introduce these transition devices in the problem situation of your story and follow up with potent key words. In subsequent scenes, you repeat these key words to remind the reader and to tie the scenes together. The success of this type of transitioning depends on how clearly and emotionally you weave the red string in the first few pages.

1. Viewpoint trait

The viewpoint trait makes an excellent transition for all patterns. In the problem situation of your story, firmly establish the trait. When you move on to subsequent scenes, remind the reader of the trait with key action words. This example shows the indecisive trait of Natalee:

> Only since Aunt Harriet's death did Natalee worry about the future. The months of probate revealed how little

financial security antiques offered. One day she decided to sell out and get a 9-5 job, and the next she changed her mind and tried to think of ways to make antiques pay more.

Each scene in the story highlights this trait, uniting the action of the entire story.

The following example shows the trait in a complication scene:

The longer the Larkins looked at her antiques, the more Natalee determined not to sell them a single item.

In the crisis the trait comes forward strongly positive.

Her way of life meant antiques. She would never feel happy in real estate or even comfortable. Even if she would never have a big bank account, she would settle for staying in the antiques business.

2. Motivation

In a character story only a solid flashback dramatically establishes the motivation for the Viewpoint's actions and reactions. Exactly as in the other devices—and as discussed in Chapter 5—the key words continue to transition motivation through all the scenes.

For Natalee, the memory of Aunt Harriet acts as the motivating transition:

Every time Kenneth brought up selling the business, she felt as if she betrayed Aunt Harriet, who had spent so much time and effort collecting these antiques. Perhaps she felt too sentimental, but this "stuff," as Kenneth called it, carried many happy memories.

In a later scene with Steve she tells him how she feels about the Tiffany vase, continuing the motivation:

"All right, I do want to keep the vase," she admitted, "because it reminds me of Aunt Harriet. She kept raising the price, too."

So even though your story needs only scattered flashback, you must still motivate your characters, as in these two examples:

> Natalee wanted to slap Mrs. Larkin's hand as she rubbed greedy fingers across the Victorian occasional table. Aunt Harriet spent three years talking the owner into selling it.

or

> Natalee stood motionless as she stared at the way Steve had arranged the booth. Aunt Harriet would never have put depression glass next to the piece of Tiffany. She must change it.

3. Single emotion

All stories rely on a dominant emotional tone as a transition. The dominant emotion of a story provides the overall reaction you want your reader to share with the Viewpoint. To create the conflict in the problem situation, the Viewpoint selects the wrong way to satisfy his desire or longing. The right and wrong approaches to the solution of the problem suggest the conflict which shows how the Viewpoint reacts as the story develops.

Love and romance dominate the emotion of the Natalee story. The reader shares Natalee's need for love whether it involves her with Steve, the right man, or with Kenneth, the wrong man. The complications give them equal play. The crisis disillusions her about Kenneth, and she reaches out to Steve.

The dominant emotion makes transitioning simple. The problem situation establishes Natalee's need for love. Transition subsequent scenes with the previous decision dictating the emotional facet. Here we do three separate transitions:

(1) From the moment she met the Crandalls, she liked them. They seemed so much in love. For the first time she felt a strange loneliness.

(2) Steve gave her the same security Aunt Harriet had provided; yet she couldn't call it the same. Aunt Harriet brought comfort. Steve created excitement.

(3) She wanted Kenneth one time to take her in his arms and talk about marriage without mentioning selling the antiques. He made her feel like a child offered a stick of candy only to have it jerked away.

Single emotion transitions greatly strengthen the impact of any story.

4. Setting

In the problem situation of your story weave the setting so vividly and dramatically through the action that you convince the reader the background has a potent influence on the Viewpoint's decision. Pull out key words for transitions.

The setting creates the problem situation in the opening of the story. In the ensuing scenes, references to specific antiques keep the setting vivid in the reader's mind. The setting actually helps in the solution of Natalee's problem.

We use two settings in the Natalee story. Let's show the action in the setting at Natalee's Victorian home:

Natalee pulled the chain on the Tiffany lamp to give the room a soft glow. Mrs. Crandall gave an audible gasp. "What a wonderful room!" She did a slow spin, trying to absorb everything.

Kenneth went over to the paneled wall to cut on the switch for the crystal chandelier. Mrs. Larkin moved over to the old china cabinet.

"I want you to especially notice this old Victorian piece," she began the sales pitch.

Little by little we introduce the various antiques in the room between character action to gradually suggest the total picture. The objects become the transitioning devices to bring the overall setting to the reader's mind. The reader then fills in the rest of the setting.

5. Pointers and plants

A *pointer* suggests the possibility of future action in a story. The following scene establishes another pointer before picking up the previous one. The process of pointing and fulfilling continues and ties your story together. Your Viewpoint thinks of what he hopes will happen when he makes a decision for action. This, too, points to future complications.

For example, Kenneth sets the date for Natalee to meet the Larkins. We point to the trouble with the station wagon. We let Steve show the reproduction vase. The Larkins bring up the Crandalls. They have left some items with the Crandalls. Steve's offer of a partnership points to the ending of getting Steve and Natalee together.

If you need an object, some facts, a group of people, or conditions of any kind you plan to use later in the story, the reader must learn about them before you put them to use. We refer to these as *plants*. New writers far too often rely on what professionals call the old rope trick.

A man climbs a cliff and finds himself marooned fifteen feet short of the crest. His fingers grow numb—no more handholds above him. He will surely fall. Suddenly in his pocket he finds a coil of rope, and then he sees a tree on the edge of the cliff. He takes out his good old rope, tosses it over the good old tree, grabs the other end and hauls himself to safety. The reader asks where did he get the rope? The professional never has his character *happen* to find a rope or a tree; he *plants* them in a previous scene, handy for the Viewpoint to use.

In the Natalee story we plant the Tiffany vase and introduce a reproduction. We plant Natalee's antiques and her Victorian home that may get Kenneth the partnership. We plant the station wagon and Steve's van, to mention a few examples.

Planting gets rid of coincidence in a story. When you plant, make sure that you pick up. Nothing so annoys the editor and the reader as a dangling plant. Make a list of the pointers and plants you will need in your story and work them into the scene summary so you don't rely on any rope tricks for your reader.

6. Gimmick-symbol

A *gimmick* provides a tangible focus as it appears from scene to scene. Natalee introduces the Tiffany vase in the opening situation. From then on we point to the fact it has not sold. In the crisis the vase helps to project the moment of revelation. In a complication scene we could mention the vase in this way:

> Natalee stared at the blue iridescent beauty of the vase. Mrs. Devereaux gave a deep sigh. "I love the tulip shape in Tiffany."

Later on we mention the vase as customers look at it. Mentions of the vase link the scenes together. Anytime you use a gimmick, build up its sentimental value so the reader will accept it as having the power to help solve the problem. Only fresh and natural gimmicks work as strong transitions. Forcing a gimmick into your story makes the plot seem contrived. The transition gimmick works best with stories emphasizing situation or situation-character.

The Viewpoint endows the *symbol* with its magical meaning. The symbol gradually takes on a spiritual meaning which the reader and the Viewpoint understand and share. In most cases the reader surmises the full meaning of the symbol before the Viewpoint does, creating suspense as to whether or not he will make the discovery. Symbol transitions work well for any pattern stressing character development.

Do not confuse Viewpoint symbolism with author symbolism. In author symbolism, popular with quality stories, the writer cries out against an existing practice or miscarriage of justice. The reader may or may not get the message.

In the short story, symbol transition follows the same pattern as that of the gimmick. Introduce the symbol with physical clarity and emotional detail in the problem situation. Each subsequent scene adds to the meaning of the symbol. The unfolding process comprises the transition.

A symbol can also transition a situation story. The character may credit the symbol with his success. In the crisis he misplaces the symbol and must work without it. He learns that he, alone, earns his success. With the situation story the symbol starts out solving an early problem and disappears when most needed at the crisis, a reverse of the use in a character story where it causes the problem and helps to solve it.

In addition to the key words as transitions, the gimmick-symbol can influence the Viewpoint in his right and wrong decisions. Earlier in the story, the way Steve gives the vase a prominent place in the exhibit influences Natalee not to get angry for combining the antiques into one exhibit. When Natalee must identify the vase, she looks at the genuine one and it influences her to give the true authentication.

7. Theme

The theme summarizes the Viewpoint's change and

the author's message in a short, forceful sentence. When you use theme as a transition device, begin with the right moral interpretation and shift to the wrong premise by the Viewpoint.

The Natalee story does not rely on theme transition, but I showed this technique of using the theme in the hook in Chapter 8. Here we use another version:

> As far back as she could remember, Aunt Harriet insisted they make *every effort to authenticate* an antique. If they couldn't authenticate it, they *frankly* told the buyer as much. *Honesty* came before *profit*. Any time they mistook a *reproduction* for the *genuine* article, they absorbed the loss. When she looked around the show and saw other dealers *passing on their errors* to buyers and *making money*, she wondered if *honesty* really did *pay dividends*.

The italicized key words link the subsequent scenes together. The following scenes show Natalee shifting back and forth between honesty and dishonesty. Any one of the key words in the above example will remind the reader of the right and wrong application of the theme as Natalee struggles to find her way.

No matter how deceptively these transitions read—as if they flowed from the typewriter with little effort—they require work. Key words must consciously trigger the reader's recall and reaction so that the scenes blend together. Theme, like the gimmick-symbol, unfolds slowly as the Viewpoint keeps trying to solve the problem. After the Viewpoint faces the moment of revelation, return to the correct moral attitude of the opening paragraph. If your story emphasizes character, tie your scenes together with theme.

In conclusion, when you transition scenes in your story, do not restrict yourself to only one of these devices. Every short story emphasizes one or two of these red-string transitions and lets the others reenforce. A character story makes the trait the dominant red string while motivation and theme support it. The detective or science fiction normally lets gimmick or setting dominate. The gothic or suspense focuses on setting. All stories use points, plants, and the dominant emotion.

To check your red-string transitions, read each scene and see if you mentioned the dominant one and at least one other. Make sure that the subordinate ones intensify the dominant transition. The red string furnishes the strong line of continuity; *paragraphing* supplies the supporting one.

Beware Those Paragraph Breaks

The mechanical breaks of paragraphing offer the reader an opportunity to put the story aside. To counteract this, you must hook your paragraphs together. To link paragraphs, part of the transition comes in the last sentence of the preceding paragraph and the remainder in the first sentence of the following one. Different devices add variety:

1. Repetition

Repetition develops an overlapping process in which you repeat exactly or synonymously a word or phrase. The word appears in the last sentence of one paragraph and in the first of the next:

> *Tomorrow* will be different, she thought, and went to sleep.
> But the *tomorrow*, Natalee discovered, turned out even worse.

Add to the emotional impact by overlapping the same thought or idea:

> "You'd sell to *anybody*," Steve said.
> "*Anybody* with the money," Natalee corrected.

Anytime you emotionally point to the next speaker in dialogue, you overlap the mood:

> Natalee blotted the perspiration from her neck and face.
> "I didn't remember this place being as warm as this," she said.

Transition by repeating the same length of sentence:

> "Sell out."
> "I can't."
> "You must."

Overlap the sound:

> The house grew *quiet*, almost too *quiet*.
> The *serene hush* magnified her footsteps to unnerving proportions.

Repeat the rhythm, fast or slow:

> Natalie ran rapidly toward the waiting people.
> Steve stayed right on her heels.

Long rambling sentences slow your rhythm. Words beginning with the same letter build rhythm. Some words have a natural rhythm; words like "ripple," "meander," "reverberating," "staccato," "symmetrical."

2. Comparison or contrast

Put the first half of the comparison or contrast in the last sentence of the paragraph. Complete the comparison or contrast in the first line of the subsequent paragraph:

> Natalee wouldn't know what to do with herself if she sold the business.
> Perhaps she would find real estate as fascinating.

3. The familiar or unfamiliar

Your material and the place in the story pattern determine whether you move from the unfamiliar to the familiar or the reverse. Whichever direction you follow, put one at the end of one paragraph and the other at the beginning of the next:

> Natalee closed the door and looked about the room so dear to her.
> How very remote and cold the world of real estate seemed.

4. Reversal

Start the train of thought going in one direction at the end of the paragraph. Then reverse the direction at the beginning of the following paragraph:

> Of course she could sell the antiques. She would price them, find a buyer, and—
> And grow so sentimental over each one she wouldn't dare sell.

5. Connectives

The lazy, unimaginative writer resorts to the connectives of nonfiction to transition for him. Such words as *consequently*, *likewise*, and *however* need no explaining for you have employed them all your writing life. But short stories need emotional writing.

Good transitioning in your story keeps the Viewpoint and the reader moving smoothly from place to place, time to time, emotion to emotion, scene to scene, and paragraph to paragraph without interruption until the end of the story.

Check all transitions in your story and rewrite the weak ones. Though your story now reads as one big adventure, you still want to give it a professional polish.

Polishing Pays Off

The amateur writes the first draft, types it, and mails it immediately to the editor. Then he wonders why he received a speedy form rejection. The professional writer holds that first draft until he has become objective and can look at the manuscript critically. Then he begins the tedious job of polishing that will make the words of the manuscript flow smoothly from one sentence to the next. You, too, can polish your manuscript by following this systematic checklist:

Start with a Checklist

The more proficient you become in short story techniques, the more revision you will do as you write the first draft of the story. Until you reach this mastery stage, you want to check for any defects or weaknesses you may have overlooked. A well-executed story plan marks the difference between the professional and the amateur. Begin your revision by taking a close look at your story's structure:

1. Structure

In the excitement of getting your story on paper, you

probably made changes in the original plot summary. To see if these changes weakened or strengthened your plot, write a brief summary of the action and compare it to the original summary you wrote. You might emphasize only the problems and the decisions, as in this example:

Problem: Natalee and Steve get assigned to same space at the antiques show, and they agree to share the spot.
Decision: Natalee leaves Steve to set up the display so she can meet Kenneth.
Problem: Kenneth wants her to help the Larkins sell the Crandalls on a decorating job.
Decision: Natalee agrees, so as to please Kenneth.

Continue in this manner until you have written a complete problem-decision summary. Make any necessary revisions if the decisions do not lead to the next problem.

This brief plot summary will also help you determine if you have chosen the best story pattern for your material. As a final check, read stories in six recent issues of the magazine you wish to sell and choose a story similar to yours. Write a brief summary of the plot and then compare it to yours. This may point out some simple adjustments you can make to improve your own plot. It also gives you a feeling for the style of the magazine and this feeds into your subconscious mind. When you write your story, you will approximate the same style.

To make sure that you have started at the best place, read through the chronological first draft of your story. You may find a more dramatic beginning for your story.

When you confront the character with a strong decision he must make within a short period of time, you actually open at the end of the problem situation. So you show the choice the character must make, then go back and develop the story chronologically. Some writers refer to this arrangement as a *story of decision*. This opening fits any strong character story.

If your story seems slow paced in the opening, select a part of the crisis scene where the major character literally hangs over the cliff and open there. While the bit of action catches and holds the reader's attention, it must not reveal too much of the crisis and weaken the overall suspense. Television has popularized this opening with a frame for stories that favor situation or situation-trait. Most writers call it the *suspense opening*.

You may choose to start at the climax of the story and give the outcome, particularly if a sympathetic character dies. The reader knows the outcome, but he wants to know what caused this ending. You'll find this arrangement in the quality and women's magazines.

Do not confuse these openings with flashback. You merely invert the chronological order of the story. To invert the order, write the story chronologically. Take scissors and cut out the few paragraphs you need as the opening frame. Retape and move these paragraphs to the beginning of the story. Write transitions to smoothly bridge the gap. Do not repeat the part you have cut out but use a summary transition.

When you feel satisfied you have the best pattern and starting point, then go over the line of suspense by asking a series of questions of the Viewpoint, such as:

Will Natalee sell the antiques business?
Will she share the booth with Steve?
Will she trust Steve to set up?
Will she meet Kenneth?
Will she tell Kenneth about the merger?

Continue in this manner until you have sketched out the entire line of suspense in your first draft. If one question does not lead logically to the next, or if you must struggle to find the next question, you have a break in the line of suspense that needs patching.

The sequence of scenes contributes to the dramatic development of your story. A shift in arrangement may add more dramatics. A reversal of a complication sometimes provides a new twist. Try new combinations by taking something from one scene and adding it to another. Make the complication the problem situation or the first complication, the second one. These changes may improve or verify the present sequence.

Each scene should contain all the essentials. Take the pages of your scene summary and read across them: all the purposes, the time, the places, the action, and the decisions. All must show forward movement. Continuity comes with each essential hooking into its counterpart in the following scenes.

Make sure that each cycle in the scene moves the action forward. Note the balance between full and bare dialogue. Have you moved from emotion to motion? Eliminate any static or repetitious speeches. The amount of conflict needs to fit the position of the scene in the sequence. Do your scenes accomplish this? If all of these structural analyses confirm you have made the best choices, then go to work on the *characters*.

2. Characters

Your characters may seem very clear to you since you created them, but they may not come alive for the reader. Begin your checking of characters with the Viewpoint. Make sure that you have projected only one trait and have blended the tags to produce the desirable gray. Can you make the trait more believable, with more identification? Does the trait keep the action moving? A writer may think of his Viewpoint as having one trait but may actually have projected him with another.

Remember, only the viewpoint changes. Have you made the change too great or too trivial for the chosen trait? Did you concentrate on only one theme, or have you implied several along the way? Does your theme summarize the change in the Viewpoint with one brief sentence?

Make sure that the trait leads directly to the theme of the story.

Does your Viewpoint act or talk in an unsympathetic manner? Then establish motivation which helps the reader to understand or at least not dislike the character. Did you over- or undermotivate?

The trait, tags, change, theme, and motivation of your Viewpoint must blend into a single image you projected to the reader. Once you have the Viewpoint in focus, the other characters must play their roles properly.

Check to see if any character steals the spotlight from the Viewpoint. The trait, function, abilities, tags, and motivation must synchronize to project the picture you want. If you read all the spoken lines of a supporting character and those of the Viewpoint, the tiniest shift in characterization becomes evident. Make sure that you projected the two characters in believable tones of gray—not in black and white.

You may want to combine minor characters or reduce some to stage property. Overlap the functions or exchange functions for a new twist. Once in a while you might want to add a character to pick up the story pace.

When you feel satisfied that you have projected the character you visualized for your story, you will then check the pace.

3. Pace

Until you complete the first draft of your story, you cannot accurately check the pace. Every short story has an up and down rhythm created by alternating fast dramatic action with slow emotional thinking by the Viewpoint. In this manner the reader experiences periods of intense stimulation followed by moments of relaxation.

A situation pattern creates a faster pace than one that stresses character. In the character story, the Viewpoint does more introspection. Consequently situation patterns have short relaxation periods, while those accenting character have longer ones. The combination situation-character falls somewhere between the two extremes.

The opening scene usually moves fast and slows toward the decision. Between each scene comes a brief letdown. The first complication moves slowly, the second faster. The third complication may speed up or slow down to a walk depending on your material. The crisis begins slowly but picks up momentum for a crescendo finish. The pace slows momentarily at the moment of revelation, then goes into fast action for the climax. While this describes the average, you always must consider your material when setting the pace of your story.

Devices for speeding up pace include flashback, bare dialogue, rapid narration, and—most of all—action. For a faster pace, you can reduce a scene to a number of incidents or to a scene substitute. Slow the pace with Viewpoint emotional thinking, full dialogue, flashback, or characterization through major character reaction. By adding more description to the setting, you reduce the speed but don't stop the story action.

Practice and experience will make pacing almost a reflex action.

4. Adjusting the length

Some writers have a tendency to overwrite and wind up with too many words. Others tend to write too briefly and need to expand.

Cutting a too long, rambling manuscript can enhance the dramatic impact and continuity. If you need to cut only a few hundred words, read the manuscript word by word and prune out the unnecessary ones or even complete sentences.

When you must cut five or more pages, eliminate an entire scene or combine two scenes. A scene substitute may provide the answer.

Substitute scattered flashback for a solid flashback. Reduce the number of conflicts within a scene. Shorten the transitions or cut out any paragraph that does not add to the dominant emotion. Eliminate a character by incorporating the functions of two. Cutting can greatly strengthen a story.

You can expand a manuscript much easier than you can cut it. Strengthen the characters and increase the projection devices, or expand the motivation. If you make the Viewpoint's problem a degree more serious, this will require new and longer complications. Add words by elaborating the setting, and give it more emotional play in the story. Dramatic incidents easily convert to scenes.

Replace some of the bare dialogue with full dialogue. Add more conflict to the scene cycle and expand the transitions between scenes. This expansion in plot, characterization, and setting could necessitate the addition of new characters—especially minor ones.

Now and then, you can use two supporting characters to offset a strong opposing one. For example—bring in the owner of the real estate firm with Kenneth to offset a stronger Steve, or bring in a dealer and close friend of the aunt as a positive influence, or bring in the promoter of the show to provide more background. Look at the list of minor motivating characters and include a theme or background character.

5. *The tape treatment*

Revision does not mean a complete retyping. Each time you type a new draft, you can easily change the general direction of the story.

Revision follows a piecemeal process. When you make the first draft, file the copy in a safe place so you can refer to it later. If a paragraph needs revision, cut out and remove the old paragraph and tape in the new one. The manuscript won't look neat, but you will maintain the original emphasis. Continue the revision in this manner, retyping only the revised portions until you complete the job. If you desire, you may eventually type a clean copy.

Take this clean or taped-and-revised copy and compare it with your original draft. Some of your original paragraphs may seem better than the revised ones. Tape them back into the manuscript. This tape treatment not only preserves the original emphasis of your story, it also saves you hours of typing. This system also works well when cutting or expanding a manuscript.

The time you save in typing you can invest in developing *style*.

Check Out Your Style

Style is your signature—it enables the reader to recognize your writing without the assistance of a by-line. While some writers use words easily, most individual styles emerge only after you have learned writing techniques so well you use them as a reflex action. Knowing the craft of writing frees you to concentrate on developing plus values.

The following suggestions will help you improve your writing style:

1. Words

Begin a romance with words. The precise word transmits a picture and a mood to the reader. To find that special word, search your memory, lifetime vocabulary, or association bank for a special emotional feeling. And don't hesitate to use a thesaurus, dictionary, or word-finder—that's what they're for: to help writers write.

Then make a list of probable words and choose the best one. The precise word can touch the reader more directly than a string of hit-and-miss adjectives, so search until you find it or them. The right words move the reader to identify and care about your major character.

2. Parts of speech

Get good mileage from the parts of speech. Nouns can stir the imagination, but only if you match them to the mood of your story and keep them specific. Each of these nouns has a special meaning: "frill," "keepsake," "bauble," "nicknack," and "bangle." Also consider such mood words as "mystic," "melancholy," "pensive."

Verbs bring action and immediacy to story conflict and character projection. A character could "skip," "race," "dawdle," "hike," "hurry," or "tiptoe."

Long strings of adjectives make the reader jumpy; he hurdles them. Let one adjective do the work of three.

Too many people overwork the word *just*, as in the phrases "just in time" or "just right." Every time you write *just*, stop and substitute one of these words:

"right," "exact," "merely," "only," "fair," "usual," "even," or "barely." Many times you do not need the just at all.

Don't overwork the adverb very. Strike it out or replace it with "greatly," "extremely," "exceedingly," or "tersely." Often you can spark your copy by inserting an action adverb. Intensify how a character speaks in dialogue, as in "he said loudly." Don't use too many adverbs or you nullify the effectiveness.

When you replace a noun with a pronoun, make sure of your reference. No other noun must come between the reference and the word it replaces. Avoid indefinite references, such as "there are" or "it was thought that." In fact, cut out all needless expression, such as "needless to point out" or "it has been found that." These reflect poor discipline in writing.

3. Sentences

The type of sentences you select will project your emotion. A short sentence depicts shock; a rambling one creates a dreamy effect. But do avoid the sentence that runs on and on for an entire page. Nothing loses the reader quicker. Never let the major character ask himself one question after another. The reader either puts the story down or skips the questions.

Sentences need simplicity and clarity of expression. Achieve variety by varying your sentence types— simple, complex, compound, exclamatory, or question. Decide on your emotional focus or conflict and choose the sentence that best performs the function. Always remember that the overuse of any single type of sentence—especially the exclamatory—lessens effectiveness.

Sentences need facts and feelings. You may put a fact in one sentence and a feeling in the next one. You can start with several factual sentences and move to a series with strong feeling for contrast.

This sentence puts the fact and feeling in one:

> Although the show would open in a matter of minutes [*fact*], Natalee wished she could wait another day to collect her confidence [*feeling*].

Balance your sentences for fact and feeling and you'll greatly improve your style.

4. Tenses

Watch your tenses. Most short stories take place in the active past.

Beginning writers have a tendency to use the present tense, which lacks the punch of the active past. Avoid, too, the weak progressive tenses, as in "*he was going*" or "*they are planning to stay.*"

Had, an auxiliary verb, refers to action in the remote past. Sprinkling your copy with *hads* removes the strong immediacy of the action verb. For this word substitute "must," "needed," "necessarily," "possessed," or "owned."

Voice also needs attention. Eliminate the passive voice and write only in the active if you want vigor and directness in your style.

These suggestions do not cover every eventuality, but they do offer you a beginning from which to expand your creativity. The more you use these devices, the more you will discover how to make your style truly your signature in your short stories.

Choosing a Title

While the writer with some success in selling need only meet the competition, the novice must surpass it to get recognized. He soon learns that outstanding titles catch an editor's attention. Most writers develop their own method of finding titles, such as questions, mystery, or shockers. But many writers prefer to search the basic elements of a short story:

1. The problem

If your story stresses situation rather than character development, study the major character's problem or the conflict action for the title. Example: "A Game of Show and Sell."

2. The character trait

When your character dominates the action of the story, the title may emphasize the name, the occupation, or the trait. Example: "Love's Decision."

3. The theme

A title may use part or all of the theme, but try to emphasize the positive facet. Example: "Love's Merry-Go-Round."

4. The setting

The setting title works best with a story where the location dominates the action of the characters or dictates the events. From this source come titles for the gothic, suspense, mystery, or detective story. Example: "Love Among the Antiques."

5. The time

Titles from this source indicate a story with a strong immediacy or a definite time span. Words such as "interlude," "hour," "year," or "day" appear in the title. Some suggest a historical period, a special year, or an event. Example: "A Day of Decision."

6. The gimmick-symbol

The title names the gimmick or the symbol if either

plays a dominant role in the story action. Example: "A Touch of Tiffany."

This gimmick-symbol title we would choose for the Natalee story.

7. The literary quotation

You can take the quotation exactly as it is and select a phrase which becomes the title. Or you may find a quotation you can individualize to your story by changing a word or two. "To lie before us like a land of love and dreams," by Matthew Arnold, for example, could become: "A Show of Love and Antiques."

8. The lucky phrase

Most writers select a *working title* to maintain continuity as they develop a story. The working title is rarely the final title, as it usually lacks the excitment and intrigue necessary to catch the reader's attention.

Completely forget choosing a final title at least until you have written the first draft of the story. Then as you polish, you may run across an apt phrase that jumps at you from the copy. May you experience such joy.

9. The imitation

When you find that none of the above sources furnishes you with a good title, then go to the magazines and read titles. Don't copy them, but they will start you thinking of similar ones. Your market research should also tell you what sorts of titles the magazine you hope to sell prefers.

An editor may suggest a likely title for your story. Many have become adept at this technique, but don't depend on such help. You want to train yourself in the art of finding titles that catch attention.

Keep your titles short, loaded with curiosity, even double meanings. Never give away too much. Let the title serve as a unifying force in your story, closely related to the characters and the action.

When you have polished your story to a luster, give it another reading for spelling, punctuation, and grammar. You now have the story ready for market.

Choosing Your Market

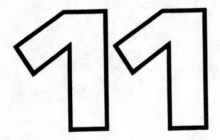

Finding the right market for your first short story demands as much work as writing it. Magazines that publish short stories buy from both new and experienced writers. Editors need newcomers to replace old pros who drop out. The appearance of new magazines in the market opens other doors for new writers. Finally, newcomers offer the fresh approach that readers demand.

The new writer, however, frequently overlooks markets he could easily sell. Special-interest and regional magazines need material, too. Although they pay less than major companies, they do offer you an opportunity to sell while you aim for the top circulation magazines.

As pointed out in the first chapter, the short story market has become highly specialized in that you write in specific categories, such as science fiction. This has expanded the market—not limited it—and made selling easier. Any writer who expects to succeed in selling short stories, however, must keep in touch with the changing market.

How to Study the Market

Any writing market demands continuous study and analysis—and especially the short story, which eternally vacillates between situation and character emphasis.

Once you establish the basic requirements of a market, you must continually update the information. A number of publications will greatly help you with the general picture of the market:

1. Books and trade journals

Most libraries can furnish you with books that list the names of the magazines that buy freelance material— their addresses, editors, requirements or needs, and rates of pay. If you plan to make a career of writing, you will want to buy a copy of a market book.

Each year Writer's Digest Books publishes Writer's Market. This book groups the markets according to science fiction, detective, religious, and so on. This same publisher also releases Writer's Yearbook, a paperback, that lists major markets. Finally, Writer's Digest, a monthly trade journal, provides current coverage on changes in market requirements and editorial policies, along with new markets.

The Writer, a similar magazine, gives about the same type of market information and prints each month information for one type of specialized market, such as the short story or the filler. This company also releases the Writer's Handbook, which classifies the current markets by categories.

Literary Market Place, published by R. R. Bowker, likewise lists market information.

You can probably find one or more of these publications in your library. But even recently released market books provide information three to four months old because of the time required for printing. Keep your market book up-to-date by subscribing to one of the monthly trade journals. Clip out any changes in market or announcements of new ones and tape to the margins or any appropriate place in your book. You may want to add an envelope pocket on the back.

To find a market classify your story as to category. If you have a suspense or mystery story, then check the magazines in this category. On a file card write the name of the magazine and the requirements the editor gives. You will then apply these general requirements to a specific magazine. Check the current writer's magazines for any changes in policies.

Suppose that you wrote your story with no specific market in mind. Try to classify it as to romance, adventure, or whatever. List the magazines whose requirements your story would fit.

The background of the story may help you with the market. A Canadian background would suggest a Canadian market. A business publication magazine would have an interest in a story dealing with a secretary or an executive. A racial background might sell a magazine that took that type of story.

Some magazines like strongly plotted stories while others buy slice-of-life or circle. Almost any editor wants good characterization. Certain religious magazines always look for gimmick or symbol in stories.

You can eliminate all of this random searching by selecting your market first and writing the story to its requirements.

2. Magazines

Follow the excellent advice of editors who suggest you read and analyze the magazine you hope to sell. First, you must find the magazine. Public libraries subscribe to a large number of magazines, and you can check out the older issues. The current issues you read in the library.

If you can't find the magazines you want in the library or on a newsstand, then write the editor and ask for sample copies. I usually send a stamped, self-addressed envelope and ask the editor to bill me for the cost. Where else can you invest a nominal sum and receive such a bonus return? At one of the local churches, you may secure copies of a denomination magazine. Many of the religious magazines will send guideline booklets.

Check among your friends as to the magazines they take and ask them to save some for you. Some thrift shops and secondhand stores sell back issues of magazines but don't buy those over a year old.

So by putting forth a little effort you can secure copies of magazines to analyze.

If a magazine publishes a large number of stories each month, you will need to analyze only three issues. If the magazine prints only two stories a month, you must read six to eight issues to get the full short story picture.

Begin your analysis of the magazines by picturing the reader. Study everything in the magazines—the features, articles, advertisements, and especially the letters to the editor. All of these combine to reveal the reader and his interests, tastes, background, needs, family situation, and other details that will help you write for the market.

Once you can picture the reader, zero in on the short stories.

You may find yourself getting carried away by the emotion in a well-written story. If so, read the story normally and then backwards. Start with the last paragraph, then the next, and so on until you reach the beginning. This method may sound ridiculous, but you will see it reveals the techniques hidden under the smooth emotional cover.

I use a basic chart that I fill in on each story. The more information you record, the easier you make writing for this magazine:

General Facts
  Title
          Length [The next chapter tells how to estimate length.]
          Pattern [such as situation, character]
          Story order [such as chronological, suspense]
          Hook [trait, setting, action]
          Single emotion [love, mystery, adventure]
          Immediacy
          Setting
          Gimmick-symbol [Indicate which, and the meaning of the symbol.]
          Viewpoint [major character, minor character]
          Number of scenes [Look for the decision points and changes in time and place.]
          Number of characters
          Plus value [Give what you think made the story sell.]
Characterization
      Viewpoint character
          Sex
          Age
          Problem
          Trait [negative and positive facet]
          Tags [negative and positive]
          Motivation
          Ability
          Change
      For each of the other characters
          Sex
          Age
          Function
          Trait

Tags
Motivation
Ability

When you have completed this information for all the stories in three to six issues of the magazine, summarize the information. Compare the titles and make deductions as to the average length, emotion, and the like. What pattern proved the most popular? Continue with this comparison until you have covered all points. This analysis should give you a complete profile on the type of story that sells the easiest to this magazine. Keeping this model in mind, tailor your next story to fit it.

From time to time you want to update this model. Select another magazine in the same category and read enough stories to make a comparison. Suppose you selected a confession magazine to analyze. You read enough of the competitor's magazine for a comparison. You, no doubt, will find few differences. No matter how slight the differences, do make note of them.

When you have analyzed the magazine you want to sell and read issues of others for comparison, make a list of where you plan to send your manuscript. You should list from three to six markets and put this information with the copy of the short story.

Help from the Pros

A number of people associated with the profession can help you and will if you show promise. Certainly a writer needs all the help he can get.

1. Editors

Editors like to discover new talent, so they take a careful second look at a manuscript by a writer who shows ability. They may mention changes and offer to take another look. Sometimes they will suggest you send it to another magazine. Other encouragement consists of including a printed form on their market requirements. This indicates you almost sold, so by all means try again.

Rejection slips certainly speak for the editor. Most magazines have a standard, printed rejection slip which bluntly states you have failed to meet the editorial requirements. If the editor scribbles "Sorry" or "Maybe next time" on it, try that editor with another story or a revision of the one submitted. With only the printed form, study the magazine stories some more to see where you missed.

Some editors have a printed letter which states your manuscript has merit in spite of the fact it does not meet the requirements of this market and invites you to submit something else. In this printed letter, the editor types in your name and address and signs his name. Send your next submittal to him.

The most encouraging rejection slip comes as a personal letter from the editor pointing out some of the defects of the story. He plainly states that if you would like to revise, he will look at it *purely on speculation.* Some editors will frankly tell you that they recently purchased a story similar to yours and suggest that you might submit it again at a later date.

When one company publishes several magazines, usually each has a different editor and you must submit separately to each of them. Sometimes one editor handles two magazines, so he considers your manuscript for both. Check in *Writer's Market* for the various policies on submitting.

Sometimes you may want to try a different group of markets. If your story has merit, you will get some comment.

2. Writing classes and organizations

Many colleges and national writer's clubs sponsor classes in writing. How valuable the class proves depends upon the instructor and the other members. If the instructor writes himself and knows *how to communicate* his knowledge of markets and requirements, choose that class. This type of instructor will attract students who want to sell or have sold to secondary markets. The ones who have sold can give you excellent, firsthand information on editorial policies, as well as on individual preferences of editors.

When you make several sales, you become eligible for a local or national writer's organization. In selecting a local group, find out about the membership. All writer's organizations emphasize helping the member. Clubs that require sales as a membership requirement may offer you more help than ones that invite anyone interested in writing to join. Use the same criteria in choosing your national organization.

Local units of national organizations often reflect the personality of the members, but you do have many advantages associated with the central headquarters. Most get out a newsletter that gives information you could receive from no other source.

Both organizations and classes offer an opportunity to brainstorm with fellow writers who can give you market information from firsthand experiences with editors. Such professionals may introduce you to visiting editors or call an editor's attention to you by letter. Writing instructors also have contacts with editors and publishers who want to meet new talent.

3. Critics

Most beginners want praise, not honest criticism. Unless you can take straightforward, constructive criticism, do not bother with a professional critic.

Critics, like writing classes and organizations, need careful investigation. Talk with several people who have used the services of the critic and find out how he has helped with sales. A good critic must objectively analyze your manuscript for specific weaknesses and give remedial directions so clearly that you can revise and sell.

A critic must consider your background and experience and let these guide him in his critique of how you have made use of your material.

To find out how well a critic gives directions, ask him for a sample of his work or the names of several clients. Check to see what he has written.

Unless you know enough about writing techniques and understand the lingo, you will have difficulty putting a critic's suggestions into practice. Let's face it, as in everything else in life, you will find both good critics and bad—so investigate carefully before you choose.

4. Writer's conferences

Notices of conferences appear in writer's magazines or in your local newspaper. Sponsors of conferences include writer's clubs, colleges, and occasionally a publishing company.

A writer's conference offers inspiration, lectures on techniques by writer-teachers, and personal contact with editors. On the program, editors give firsthand information on the needs of magazines, and some even distribute guidebooks on how to write for them

More and more conferences offer private consultation with an editor-in-attendance to discuss your story. Do not overlook the value of association with other conferees, since many selling writers attend these conferences. At informal and unscheduled sessions, you can pick up a great deal of market information.

When you select a conference, do evaluate the staff, and check on private consultations and workshops offered. Look at the conference analytically and choose the one which offers the most direct opportunities to develop you as a writer.

5. Agents

Every unpublished writer dreams of a good agent who can sell everything—especially the terribly amateur story. An agent does not work miracles. He can sell only what you can. A reputable agent takes only ten percent of what he sells for you; consequently he cannot afford to accept you as a client unless you sell regularly.

In 1928, a group of literary agents organized the Society of Author's Representatives and set standards of operation. You would want one of these agents, so secure a list of membership from Authors Guild, 234 West 44th Street, New York, New York 10036.

Services vary with the agent, the size of the agency, his experience, and his publishing contacts. He agrees to offer for sale such manuscripts as he believes publishable. He may or may not offer editorial advice on form or content. Do not think of him as a writing instructor, rewrite man, or critic. He selects the best markets for the material, negotiates the terms of sale, collects the money, and handles any other literary property rights.

The agents I know personally have only verbal agreements which either the client or the agent may terminate at any time. An agent does not advertise his services, nor does he charge the author for expenses incurred in submitting the manuscript. Some do charge reading fees for unsolicited material but refund this in the event of a sale.

In recent years some of the big agencies have decided to focus chiefly on the sale of books, movies, and television. Books bring in more money because the agent can offer them at auction to the highest bidder for hardback and paperback rights. You can find out if the agent handles the short story by writing him or, if you know one of his clients, ask that person.

From time to time magazines announce that they will buy only from agents, but most markets do buy directly from freelance writers.

You may secure an agent in several ways once you begin selling regularly to national markets. Contact the agent directly and send him a resume of what you have sold. Offer to submit copies of published stories and an unpublished one. Do send him a good story—not one that has already been submitted and rejected several times.

Sometimes at writer's conferences or functions you meet a professional who offers to recommend you to his agent. This does not guarantee a reputable agent or acceptance. The agent may accept you as a client, recommend another one, or refuse to represent you.

When you sell several stories to an editor, you might ask for a recommendation to an agent. If your by-line appears regularly in several national magazines, an agent may contact you. Choose your agent very carefully and make sure the name appears on the recommended list. Otherwise, work without an agent.

Keep Tabs on a Changing Market

The writer must learn to recognize trends in the market and take advantage of them. Market trends change with the social, economic and political outlook of our nation. Since the market has changed from general to specialized magazines, this has resulted in several other trends:

1. Science fiction

Science fiction magazines have expanded greatly and are attracting a wide variety of readers. These discerning readers want good plots, believable characterization, and unique settings.

Science fiction depends strongly on the art of believable detail. A basic knowledge of science has always helped writers, but careful research and a vivid imagination more than equalizes for those who do not have this specialized background.

You will find two types of markets: the magazine and the anthology in paperback. The anthologies come out under continuing general titles. The series anthology contains a collection of well-written but unrelated science fiction original stories. The theme anthology includes stories that relate to the same cental idea.

2. Confessions

At one time more than thirty confession magazines bought a large number of stories, but television soap operas stole their readers. Then the pill played havoc with the unwed-mother story. Some confession magazines have gone erotic, while others now deal with such once-tabooed problems as racial prejudice, divorce, or incest. Perhaps the most noticeable trend has been the rise of black confessions. Occasionally you will find a light humorous story or one dealing with the mystic or occult.

The market appears now in the middle of a comeback.

3. Detective murder mystery

The stories have divided into these types: the detective or one accused finding the murderer, the locked-room mystery or puzzler, and the psychological mystery where the major character finds the murderer by using psychology. In the last type, the reader knows the murderer, and the suspense comes with how the detective will find him. Occasionally you will find a story involving the supernatural. With the push of women's liberation, look for women to become the crime solvers. Female major characters have already appeared in the mystery novel.

This market has held its own.

4. Religious magazines

The stories in this market show a predominance of love for mankind as the central idea. They seem to show stronger characterization, with emphasis on the little person or follower rather than on leaders or important people.

Since each denomination approaches life a little differently, you will need to carefully read the magazine and talk with members of the church that publishes it to learn any special Christian beliefs. You'll find local ministers most helpful. The stories always emphasize a Christian theme but do not necessarily read preachy or churchy.

5. Quality magazines

The literary market has always placed emphasis on quality rather than quantity. The top general interest magazines in this category have decreased the amount of fiction they print. A number of new magazines have joined the ranks of the small literary publishers to increase the marketing opportunitites for quality short story writers.

6. Westerns

This market has grown quite lean for short stories

because of strong competition. Readers seem more interested in the abundance of true and historical stories about the West that nonfiction magazines publish than in fictionalized accounts. Others find watching westerns on television or at the movies more exciting than reading them.

Anthology collections of western stories do appear in paperback on the magazine stand. The writers of the western short story have for the most part moved on to the paperback novel.

7. Women's magazines

The magazines group themselves into three categories: those for the career-oriented woman, those for the family woman, and those which cover both types of women. The circle plot to present a light humorous story, and the slice-of-life for a serious family problem have been adapted from the quality market.

To compete with the personal experience article, stories tend to deal more with reader-identification problems than with escapism, such as the loss of a child, divorce, the loss of a husband, and the working woman, to name a few. Love and romance still remain the most popular themes.

While love and romance dominate, the change has come in the type of story, which now includes suspense, mystic, horror, and even the supernatural. Occasionally you read a nostalgic story that closely resembles an article. This market seems determined to win back the readers that personal experience, nostalgic, and humor articles have enticed away.

8. Men's magazines

This market has moved steadily toward erotica, with sex—in some form or another—dominating. One writer for this market divides it into two groups: quality erotica for the higher paying markets and raw erotica for the lesser paying ones. The erotica may appear in all types of fiction: fantasy, humor, adventure, science fiction, horror, mystery, satire, social realism, or the psychological drama. I even found a western in one magazine.

This chapter covers only the general trends in the specific categories, but you can easily fill in the details with a little reading and research. Keeping up with the changing market covers only one part of the business of writing.

The Business of Short Story Writing

Writing, like any other profession, has its own business procedures and practices. Unless you follow them, you instantly mark yourself as an amateur. Professionalism begins with the preparation of your final manuscript.

Preparing Your Manuscript

To prepare your manuscript for the editor, you need certain operating equipment and supplies, and must follow certain procedures:

1. Equipment

If you do not own a typewriter, then borrow, rent, or buy one. Editors prefer pica (standard) type rather than elite. If you already own a machine with elite or script type—both difficult to read—buy the next one with pica. *Always type double-space any manuscript you send to an editor.*

Although you may begin writing by putting the typewriter on the kitchen table or on a stand of some sort, eventually you will need a desk and a file cabinet if you continue to write. A desk scale for weighing your manuscripts and a booklet or chart of up-to-date postal rates saves numerous trips to the post office.

Books for your library also become a part of your standard equipment: dictionary, thesaurus, style book, quotation book, English grammar, to mention only the basic ones. Any book on writing techniques, marketing, or vocabulary building will improve your production. So start now to build your library around your personal writing needs.

2. Supplies

Every writer looks for ways to cut the cost of supplies. Perhaps these suggestions will help you:

More and more editors join the list of those who do not like erasable bond, since it smears and proves difficult to write on. Instead of upsetting the editor, substitute 16-pound or 20-pound bond with at least 25 percent rag content. The rag content will take erasures and not show. The 20-pound, however, will wrinkle or curl less than 16-pound, but the heavier weight costs more to mail. Some writers have located a printer who will sell them a ream of rag paper in the large newspaper size and will cut it to 8½x11 inches, the standard. This works out to about 2,000 sheets and costs considerably less than buying prepackaged paper.

Buy a cheaper paper for rough drafts. Some writers find that newsprint works very well. Buy this from a printer and have it cut to the standard size. A few printers have it already cut and packaged in paper—not boxes. By watching sales at discount houses, you may buy 500 sheets of cheap typing paper for less than the cost of newsprint.

Along with everything else, carbon paper has risen in cost, too. Choose a medium weight for making more copies. Do consider xeroxing the manuscript as less messy and more convenient than using carbon. Do check on discount copy shops. In my area, some savings and loan companies allow you to duplicate 10-15 copies when you maintain a certain balance in your account. If you prefer to make carbon copies, buy your supply in bulk. Many office suppliers have their own carbon that costs less than the boxed.

Always keep a copy of your manuscript in case the original gets lost in the mail or at the publisher. Send only the original to the editor.

As a writer you should order printed stationery. In most cases your name, address, and telephone number suffice. Order at least a ream of the standard 8½x11 printed and the same amount of matching plain sheets. A ream of half sheets works well for quick notes. Lots smaller than a ream cost more.

Do order matching envelopes in legal and letter size. Printers sometimes have paper left over from other jobs and will sell you this at a great discount. Do ask your printer about this. By all means order some printed address labels that you can stick on your manuscript envelope.

You will need mailing manila envelopes in sizes 9x12 and 9½x12½ so that you can fit one inside the other. You save money when you buy a full box. Depending on your need, you may want to stock manila envelopes in legal and half size. In addition to envelopes you may want file folders which you also buy as packaged.

When you buy typing ribbons by the dozen, you get a discount. Choose cotton, nylon, film, or whatever ribbon works best with your typewriter. Do make sure that you get the dark or heavily inked ones. At the same time, consider buying cellophane tape by the dozen for the discount. Some office suppliers will give you a tape dispenser with the purchase of two dozen fillers. Constantly look for such bargains.

Under paper or office supplies, you may find a wholesale company in the yellow pages. Most paper wholesalers carry office supplies, too. These suppliers do sell to individuals but may require a minimum purchase. In this case, get several of your writing friends to buy with you.

From the post office buy a supply of postal cards. You will find many duties for them. As a convenience I buy two rolls of stamps for my holders: one for the first ounce and one for the rest.

3. Appearance and format

The typewritten appearance of your manuscript offers the editor his first impression of you. Erase but do not strike over or out. Use black ribbon and clean your keys. Let your manuscript speak for you in clean, readable, and accurate type.

Most writers do not use a title sheet. To make one, you type the title of your story in capital letters in the center of the page, halfway from the top. In the lower right-hand corner put your name and address, single-spaced in small letters. You may prefer to center this at the bottom of the page. If you use a pen name, put it under the title with a by. Place your real name at the bottom of the page.

On the first page of your manuscript put your name and address in the upper left-hand corner, single-spaced and about an inch from the top edge of the sheet. In the right-hand third of the paper and three spaces down from your name and address, write the number of words. Round off to the nearest 100.

To estimate wordage, measure three inches of an average page and count the number of words in each inch. Add these and divide by three to get the average number of words per inch. Measure the number of inches in three separate pages. Multiply this figure by the average words per inch and divide by three. This gives the average words per page. To find the total words, multiply the average per page by the number of pages.

Center your title in capitals one third of the way down your page. Two spaces below your title, center by and your name or pseudonym. Skip three spaces to begin the copy. Indent ten spaces for paragraphs. The margins of the manuscript should measure 1¼ inches on all sides of each full page. The top of the first page deviates from the 1¼ inches. Number the first page in the center at the bottom. The top of your first page will look like this:

```
John Doe
1020 River Street
San Francisco, CA   94072


                                    3,000 words



                  TITLE OF THE STORY
                       by Name
```

On each of the following pages maintain the 1¼-inch margin. In the upper left-hand corner, one inch from the edge, type your name and a key word from the title.

Come down two spaces and type the page number on the right side. Skip three spaces and begin the copy, as in this example:

```
Doe--Tiffany

2


Begin copy at this point.
```

On the last page of your manuscript put *The End* two or three spaces below the last line. Then repeat your name and address three spaces below the end but against the left-hand margin. The editor now has your name and address on two separate pages.

4. Mailing

Mail your manuscript flat in the larger manila envelope, using an address label. The smaller envelope, addressed to yourself with correct postage, fits neatly into the larger one and provides for the return trip—if necessary. By all means enclose a self-addressed postcard with the title of the story and the name of the magazine. The editor will drop it in the mail and let you know he has your manuscript. When the postcard returns, file it with the copy of your manuscript. If the editor holds your manuscript longer than four months without a decision or a letter, write and inquire but include a self-addressed stamped envelope.

Any time you use background material which adds a plus value to the story and which you personally experienced, include a brief letter verifying this technical information. Except in this one and only situation, do not burden your editor with a letter.

When you mail your manuscript, make out a file card or a notation in a loose-leaf notebook. List the name of the publisher and the date sent. If the manuscript gets rejected, fill in the date returned and clip the rejection slip to the card or the page to refer to later when you decide to do revision.

In your market research you chose six possible markets. Unless an editor asks for a revision, put your manuscript back in the mail immediately to the next magazine on the list.

The post office will advise you on rates and can supply you with a pamphlet on costs per ounce. You may send your manuscript first class or special fourth class rate. While first class costs more, it often makes sense: it assures better handling and faster delivery, especially for a manuscript the size of a story. Most first class mail sent a long distance goes airmail.

Special fourth class mail receives the same handling as parcel post, but you can only insure the manuscript for the cost of paper and typing. The post office will forward first class mail but not special fourth class. To make sure you get your manuscript back if undeliverable, put "Return Postage Guaranteed" under your return address. If you enclose a personal letter with a manuscript sent special fourth class rate, you must pay first class postage for it. Do mark "first class letter enclosed."

Do not bind your manuscript in any way or add a cover. Omit the paper clip. Any manuscript over four pages you mail flat. Under four pages, you can fold in half. Following these rules marks you as a professional.

Good Work Habits Pay Off

No one can tell any writer how many hours to work or when to schedule his time. A work schedule must fit the individual. But organized work habits do permit you to achieve maximum production for the time employed. Most writers think of work in terms of units rather than in daily hours at the typewriter, and they arrange the schedule to cover certain types of work:

1. *Planning time*

Planning time refers to work done on the story organization such as outlining the plot, sketching the characters, deciding on the setting, and other construction details. Many writers put in so much planning time that when they sit down at the typewriter to do the first draft, they do a copy which needs little revision. This professional approach, however, comes after many years of practice. The newcomer cannot expect to write a short story—even a natural—first draft, but experience and practice will reduce the necessary amount of revision.

Like other writers you may want to do planning time at the typewriter. A few prefer longhand at this stage of the story. Start your planning by generating an idea and expressing it in a three-sentence summary.

From this idea you develop the tentative plot and the characters to carry the action. Sometimes you will write a biography of each character, giving his background, likes and dislikes, abilities, trait, tags, and motivation. Planning ends when you have blocked out the scenes of your story and prepare to write the first draft. Sometimes you interrupt your planning time to do research.

2. *Research time*

A trip to the library may provide more about the

gimmick or the setting. Always do your research before you fill in the final details on your worksheet. You may want to check on themes, titles, or nonfiction articles that cover facts relative to your story.

The type of research you do depends to a large degree on your story. You may want to check with a friend in police work about some procedure for a detective story or on a scientific process you plan to write into a science fiction story. Impeccable research will quickly bring recognition and kudos from editors. In market research read the stories from a magazine you wish to sell shortly before you begin the first draft. These stories subconsciously guide you in writing your own. Occasionally you will need some specific research after you complete the first draft.

3. Typewriter time

Typewriter time includes creating the first and copying the final draft of your story. Again, some writers do this first draft in longhand. Assign yourself a quota of pages to do each day. This quota may vary from three to five pages, depending on whether you write full- or only part-time. Through experience you will learn how much time you need to meet your individual quota. Keep your schedule flexible until you can estimate the necessary time accurately. Once you establish a workable quota, strive to maintain it.

Some writers find that doing the organizing for the next session's quota makes returning to the typewriter much easier. Your quota time applies only to creating the original draft, as you want to avoid tired thinking. In revising your first draft, you can work as long as the results satisfy you or as your time schedule allows.

Always make a copy of your first draft so you can refer to it when you correct the original. If you wander from the original story line, the copy will bring you back.

Before you start revision, put this draft aside for several days so you can become more objective. Cut out the portions that need revision or polishing and tape in the correction.

4. Refueling time

When you begin to write, you feel so overstocked with ideas that you think you will never get them on paper. Eventually the supply becomes depleted. You want to think of tomorrow by daily replenishing your supply of ideas.

Refueling time includes every minute of the day that you don't write. Housewives make good writers because they can think about their stories while they vacuum or wash the dishes. Carry a small notebook and pencil with you wherever you go. When you react sensitively to a person, place or thing, list the item in your notebook.

Utilize spare minutes during the day to transfer items from your notebook to a file box so that you do not overload your memory. No one can depend entirely on memory, but you can depend on notes. As you collect items, file them on cards under appropriate divisions: title, theme, tag, trait, problem, gimmicks, symbols, names, setting. No doubt you will add other sections. When you use a card from the file, put it under *dormant* to recall later in a different combination. As you begin a new story, go through your file box for excellent help.

Learn to accumulate several short stories at the same time. When you can summarize an idea in three sentences, put this in a file folder. Add anything you can on plot, setting, or character. Each time you find something pertinent to the idea, put it in the folder. You may find a published article that will shortcut research, a picture of a person that resembles the character you have in mind. A news item might suggest a complication. Give each short story folder a tentative title.

You will know when to start planning the details of the story in preparation for writing the first draft. When you remove one folder to build into a short story, replace it with a new one. In this way you never run out of stories to write.

5. Record keeping

In addition to keeping a submittal record, you will need an accounting system for income tax purposes. Social Security defines a self-employed writer as any one earning a net of $400 in one year. Net means taking the allowable deductions. You must keep records to show your expenses.

Start your record keeping with a calendar, 9x6 inches with four or five lined spaces to make notes. On it you will record your day-by-day expenses, such as buying stamps or going to the library.

From this calendar you will record your expenses in a loose-leaf ledger. These headings will cover most of your expenses: automobile, material and supplies, dues and subscriptions, office, postage, professional and possibly research travel.

You may follow either of two methods to determine your automobile expenses. Record on your calendar the number of miles you drive in relation to your writing: going to the post office, buying supplies, research at the library. At the end of the year add all expenses that you have incurred on the car: license, gasoline, insurance, battery, tune-up, and so on. Divide the total number of miles you drove the car by the number you used it for writing. This gives you the percentage you can take for your automobile expenses.

The simpler method consists of totaling the number of miles for writing and multiplying that by the rate the government allows its employees. Test both methods and choose the one that gives you the greater deduction.

Under dues you include any club that helps you with your writing. Dues to a camping club become deductible if you use this background in your stories. All magazine subscriptions you can deduct provided they help you market your short stories. Save all receipts and keep a record of subscriptions.

Material and supplies covers anything used in your writing. You may deduct the cost of books on writing, paper, pencils—you name it. I keep all receipts in an envelope clipped to this page in the ledger.

Under office expenses come repairs on your typewriter or other equipment. To charge off a room in your home, you take the value of your house and divide this by the years of the mortgage (if 25 or 30) or by the useful life expectancy of the house. This figure gives you the yearly rate. If you have eight rooms in your home, then take one-eighth of this yearly rate for your rent. Likewise you will deduct the same percentage for utilities and insurance. Don't forget to take depreciation. If you rent, then you take advantage of your monthly payments. Remember, you must use this room exclusively for writing.

Since postage amounts to such a very large expense for the writer, place it in a separate category. The post office will give you a receipt when you buy stamps or mail a manuscript special delivery or registered.

The Internal Revenue Service has become very strict about some of the things placed under professional expenses. Include here fees paid an agent or a critic, cost of a class in writing, or attendance at a writer's conference. If you can't find a place for expenses related to writing under any other category, it may fit here.

Writers do make an entry for research travel separate from automobile expenses. If you visit a place and sell a short story in this background, then you deduct the cost of the research travel. This provision, however, applies more to the person doing a novel or a nonfiction book. The IRS has set rules about research travel, so do check with the agency, particularly if you made the trip for pleasure, too.

Suppose that you don't make $400 net a year. Then you deduct any expenses incurred in writing the story and report for income only the remainder. You cannot take off the room in your home or any of the other deductions.

That Check Will Come!

The business of writing consists of getting ideas, packaging them, and selling on a competitive market. The sooner you approach writing with this attitude, the quicker you sell. Never doubt that writing demands hard work, but in no other field can a newcomer make such rapid strides, regardless of age, and with such excellent pay in money and personal satisfaction.

No doubt, as you start your next story, you will wonder why you needed someone to point out all these obvious fundamentals of writing. Wait! Techniques never seem obvious to a beginner. In writing, like any other learning process, you overemotionalize or underproject while you search for the correct balance. Every writer must develop through experience the emotional "feel" for proportions.

But soon you will get the "hang" of writing, and

technique becomes an automatic reflex that makes writing a joy. Errors you didn't notice before now jump at you. In fact, you will look at previous stories you wrote with a touch of embarrassment and probably wonder, "Why did I ever think I could sell when I didn't know the craft of writing?" When you reach this state of mind, you have the professional attitude essential to becoming a good writer.

So treat the story you have developed to your best individual style and send it to an editor. Begin work immediately on another. If you keep working and submitting, very soon a check will arrive in the mail. "I did it!" you shout. "I sold a short story and I can do it again." You certainly can!

Index

Other Books Of Interest

General Writing Books

Beginning Writer's Answer Book, edited by Polking and Bloss, $14.95

Getting the Words Right: How to Revise, Edit, and Rewrite, by Theodore A. Rees Cheney $13.95

How to Become a Bestselling Author, by Stan Corwin, $14.95

Make Every Word Count, by Gary Provost (paper) $7.95

Writer's Encyclopedia, edited by Kirk Polking $19.95

Writer's Market, $18.95

Writer's Resource Guide, edited by Bernadine Clark $16.95

Writing for the Joy of It, by Leonard Knott $11.95

Writing From the Inside Out, by Charlotte Edwards (paper) $9.95

Magazine/News Writing

Complete Guide to Writing Nonfiction, edited by Glen Evans $24.95

Magazine Writing: The Inside Angle, by Art Spikol $12.95

Write On Target, by Connie Emerson $12.95

Fiction Writing

Fiction Is Folks: How to Create Unforgettable Characters, by Robert Newton Peck $11.95

Fiction Writer's Market, edited by Jean Fredette $17.95

Handbook of Short Story Writing, edited by Dickson and Smythe (paper) $6.95

Writing Romance Fiction—For Love and Money, by Helene Schellenberg Barnhart $14.95

Writing the Novel: From Plot to Print, by Lawrence Block $10.95

Special Interest Writing Books

Children's Picture Book: How to Write It, How to Sell It, by Ellen E.M. Roberts $17.95

Complete Book of Scriptwriting, by J. Michael Straczynski $14.95

Complete Guide to Greeting Card Writing, edited by Larry Sandman (paper) $7.95

Complete Guide to Writing Software User Manuals, by Brad McGehee (paper) $14.95

How to Make Money Writing . . . Fillers, by Connie Emerson $12.95

How to Write a Cookbook and Get It Published, by Sara Pitzer, $15.95

How to Write a Play, by Raymond Hull $13.95

How to Write & Sell (Your Sense of) Humor, by Gene Perret $12.95

Poet's Handbook, by Judson Jerome $11.95

Programmer's Market, edited by Brad McGehee (paper) $16.95

Travel Writer's Handbook, by Louise Zobel (paper) $8.95

Writing to Inspire, by Gentz, Roddy, et al $14.95

The Writing Business

Complete Handbook for Freelance Writers, by Kay Cassill $14.95

Freelance Jobs for Writers, edited by Kirk Polking (paper) $7.95

How You Can Make $20,000 a Year Writing, by Nancy Edmonds Hanson (paper) $6.95

To order directly from the publisher, include $1.50 postage and handling for 1 book and 50¢ for each additional book. Allow 30 days for delivery.

Writer's Digest Books, Dept. B, 9933 Alliance Rd., Cincinnati OH 45242
Prices subject to change without notice.